Studies in Comparative W

The rise and fall of the plantation complex

The rise and fall of the plantation complex

ESSAYS IN ATLANTIC HISTORY

PHILIP D. CURTIN
The Johns Hopkins University

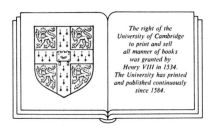

The right of the
University of Cambridge
to print and sell
all manner of books
was granted by
Henry VIII in 1534.
The University has printed
and published continuously
since 1584.

CAMBRIDGE UNIVERSITY PRESS
Cambridge
New York   Port Chester   Melbourne   Sydney

Published by the Press Syndicate of the University of Cambridge
The Pitt Building, Trumpington Street, Cambridge CB2 1RP
40 West 20th Street, New York, NY 10011, USA
10 Stamford Road, Oakleigh, Melbourne 3166, Australia

First published 1990
Reprinted 1991

Printed in Canada

Library of Congress Cataloging-in-Publication Data

Curtin, Philip D.
The rise and fall of the plantation complex : essays in Atlantic
history / Philip D. Curtin.
p. cm. – (Studies in comparative world history)
Includes bibliographies.
ISBN 0-521-37475-8. – ISBN 0-521-37616-5 (pbk.)
1. Slavery – America – History. 2. America – Social conditions.
3. Plantation life – America – History. I. Title. II. Series.
HT1048.C87   1990   89–33229
306.3'62'0973 – dc20   CIP

British Library Cataloguing in Publication Data
Curtin, Philip D. (Philip DeArmond)
The rise and fall of the plantation complex: essays
in Atlantic history. – (Studies in comparative world
history)
1. Slave trade, history
I. Title II. Series
382'.44'09

ISBN 0-521-37475-8 hardback
ISBN 0-521-37616-5 paperback

Contents

v

Aftermath

Contents

Preface

The plantation complex was an economic and political order centering on slave plantations in the New World tropics. During the century centered on about 1800, these plantations played an extremely important role in the European-dominated portion of the world economy. Though the core of the complex was the slave plantations growing tropical staples, the system had much broader ramifications. Political control lay in Europe. Much of the labor force came from Africa, though some came from Amerindian societies on the South American mainland. In a final phase in the middle to late nineteenth century, most of the labor was to come from India and China. At its peak, many of the trade goods to buy African slaves came from India, and silver to buy these same Indian goods came from mainland South America. Northern North America and Europe were important trading partners, supplying timber and food to the plantations and consuming the sugar, rum, indigo, coffee, and cotton they produced.

The origins of this economic complex lay much further back in time. Its earliest clear forerunner was the group of plantations that began growing cane sugar in the eastern Mediterranean at the time of the European Crusades into the Levant. These plantations, like their successors, produced mainly for a distant market in Europe, thus becoming the center for a widespread commercial network to bring in labor and supplies and to carry off the finished product.

With the passage of time, the heart of the complex moved

westward by way of the Atlantic islands, Brazil, and the Caribbean. It ultimately stretched from Rio Grande do Sul in southern
Brazil to the Mason-Dixon line, and it had outliers, even at its
eighteenth-century prime, on the Indian Ocean islands of Réunion
and Mauritius.[1] Later on it spread even more widely to Peru,
Hawaii, Queensland, Fiji, Zanzibar, and Natal – among other
places – but this worldwide dispersion during the nineteenth
century took place just as the complex began to be dismantled –
first with the ending of the slave trade from Africa, then with the
widespread emancipation of slaves throughout the tropical world
under European control. The plantation complex was therefore
much more than an economic order for the tropical Americas
alone; it had an important place in world history at large, and the
object of this book is to set it in this world historical perspective.
Historians of the medieval Mediterranean, of Africa, of Latin
America, of Europe, and of the United States all deal with parts
or aspects of the complex, but they rarely try to see it as a whole.

For specialists in these fields of history, some of what I have to
say will no doubt seem superficial and elementary. The plantation
complex is nevertheless an interrelated aggregate of human
experience that deserves investigation as an entity. These essays,
however, are not a textbook-like survey. A narrative general
history of the plantation complex would require a book many
times the size of this one. Instead, each essay deals with some
aspect of the complex from the perspective of world history.

These essays also have a central core of intent. The North
American segment of the plantation complex is hard to understand if it is merely seen in the context of U.S. history. The origins
of the plantation complex antedate Columbus's voyages, and it
lasted elsewhere long after its end in the United States as an
aftermath of the Civil War. Its geographical reach extended to five

---

[1] In some earlier writing, I used the term "South Atlantic system" for the same set of
institutions and interrelations I now prefer to call the "plantation complex." The reasons
for the change are two. First, the plantation complex was not really associated with the
South Atlantic in the nautical sense of that term – from the equator to Antarctica. It was
centered in the tropical world, both north and south of the equator. Second, the
intellectual world of the social sciences has been introduced in recent years to a variety
of "world systems." The plantation complex was not a "system" or a "world" in the sense
of any of those theoretical constructs. I am consciously using a less theory-laden word.

continents. These essays have little to say about slave plantations of the American South, which are familiar in any case, but it is hoped that Americans may profit from seeing aspects of their history from a broader perspective.

Because these are essays, not based fundamentally on new archival research, they are only lightly footnoted, though the "Suggestions for Further Reading" contain most of the substantive information on which the essays were based – sometimes seen from a different point of view.

I am grateful for the financial support of the Carnegie Corporation of New York to the Program in Comparative Tropical History at the University of Wisconsin, where many of the ideas presented here were first developed, and to the John D. and Catherine T. MacArthur Foundation for financial support through a Prize Fellowship during the period in which they were put into their present form. I am even more indebted to the generosity of friends and colleagues who donated their time and thought in criticizing parts or the whole of this work – especially to Anne G. Curtin, Stanley Engerman, Richard Kagan, Franklin Knight, and A.J.R. Russell-Wood. The services of the Interlibrary Loan Department of the Milton S. Eisenhower Library at the Johns Hopkins University have been as efficient and invaluable as always.

Beginnings

1

The Mediterranean origins

Europe's involvement in the plantation complex began when it encountered sugar in the eastern Mediterranean at the time of the Crusades. That encounter was, in turn, part of a larger pattern in world agricultural history. As human intercommunication grew, crops originating in one place spread to others where they could be grown. With regular contact between the Mediterranean basin and Mesopotamia, for example, date palms originally from Mesopotamia began to be grown wherever hot weather, low rainfall, and irrigation water were found together – as far west as southern Morocco.

With the rise of Islam after about 700 A.D., the old intercommunicating zone of the Indian Ocean came into much closer contact with the southern Mediterranean. As a result, a whole range of new crops from the Asian tropics began to be grown in the Mediterranean basin. Many of them came originally from Southeast Asia, though modified through several centuries of residence in India. The list includes rice, colocasia (taro or cocoyams), coconuts, sorrel, sour oranges, lemons and limes – probably sugarcane, plantains, bananas, and mangoes as well, though these may have originated in India.[1] Taken together, these and other originally tropical crops from sub-Saharan Africa had a profound influence on the economic geography of the Mediter-

---

[1] Andrew M. Watson, *Agricultural Innovation in the Early Islamic World: The Diffusion of Crops and Farming Techniques, 700–1100* (Cambridge: Cambridge University Press, 1983).

ranean, not only on the Muslim south shore. In time, many of these crops could be grown in Christian Europe by diffusion through Cyprus, Sicily, Spain, and Portugal, though much of this diffusion came only in the fifteenth and sixteenth centuries.

Sugar planting

Europe's contact with sugarcane began at the time of the Crusades, Europe's first intense contact with the Muslim world. It was an impressive discovery for people whose only source of sugar was honey. Europeans first began to import sugar from the Levant. Then, in the late eleventh and early twelfth centuries, they gained control of territory in the Levant itself, where Muslim sugar production already flourished.

Sugarcane is a crop with its own physical and economic peculiarities. Production is extremely labor intensive. Before modern machinery was available, a common rule of thumb was one worker for each acre cultivated. The weight and bulk of the harvested cane are enormous compared to those of other grasses, like wheat or maize. This meant that it was very costly to haul it any distance without first concentrating the sugar by squeezing out the cane juice and boiling it to drive off excess water, producing crystalline sugar and molasses. Every early cane farm, even one with only 100 to 500 acres of land, therefore had to have its own sugar factory to concentrate the product for shipment, though cane could be brought further to a central factory once the cost of road haulage was reduced.

Once concentrated, cane sugar products had a high value-to-bulk ratio. This meant that they could be transported for long distances, especially by relatively cheap water transport, and still sold at a profit. Economically, therefore, sugar could enter long-distance trade over far greater distances than wheat, rice, or other starchy staples in common use. But sugar also differed nutritionally from these other sources of carbohydrates. Wheat, rice, maize, potatoes, and manioc, among others, normally supplied more than half of the total nutritional intake in preindustrial societies. They took a proportionate part of society's agriculture effort at a time when the vast majority of the population worked the land. Sugar did not play that nutritional role. It could act as a supplement, but it could not provide most of the calories in a healthy diet. Without export outlets, it could only be a very minor crop for local use. Dates are a similar crop, with a very high yield and a limited nutritional role. Both sugar and dates have been associated historically with the development of long-distance trade.[2]

The Crusaders' first effort to increase sugar production to serve the European market apparently began near Tyre, conquered by the Europeans in 1123 A.D. Here the Venetians, who had taken part in the conquest, received some 21 out of the 114 conquered villages, as well as a few additional pieces of territory in northern Lebanon. Rather than letting out their villages on feudal tenures, the Venetians converted several of them to sugar production, adopting Muslim sugar technology and capitalizing on their own maritime ability to get the sugar to European markets. Other Crusaders with an eye to business also began to enter the sugar trade. Baldwin II, king of Jerusalem, had sugar works near Acre. Crusading orders like the Teutonic Knights and the Knights Templar set up sugar plantations near Tripoli, now in northern Lebanon.

Meanwhile, the Normans were moving into southern Italy and Sicily. They too found that sugar had been a developed crop under their Muslim predecessors. They continued to produce sugar, with a flurry of activity around Palermo; but the Sicilian industry was technologically backward, and it declined to virtual disappearance in the thirteenth and fourteenth centuries. The important source of sugar was still the eastern Mediterranean. Toward the second half of the fifteenth century the industry revived, and Sicily became the technological center and an important stepping stone for the transmission of sugar planting from the eastern Mediterranean to the Atlantic.

Cyprus

From the thirteenth century well into the fifteenth, Cyprus was the main center for the production of sugar consumed in Europe. With

[2]Philip D. Curtin, *Cross-Cultural Trade in World History* (New York: Cambridge University Press, 1984), pp. 21–4.

the end of the Crusades and the successful Muslim reconquest of the Levant, Levantine plantations served the Muslim world. Cyprus had been something of a side issue to the main business of the Crusades. Christians captured it in the Second Crusade. Control passed to Guy de Lusignan in 1190. He had briefly been king of Jerusalem, but he and his successors now became the feudal lords of Cyprus. They controlled it down to 1498, when it passed to Venice. During this comparatively long period, sugar production under Western control had a chance to develop institutional forms that would serve as precedents once the industry began to move on to newer fields.

These institutions differed a good deal from northern European practices that the Crusaders would have known at home. There the feudal class was a military class, not a group of agricultural estate managers. Agricultural production above the family level was organized through the village, but no one managed village agriculture in detail. Villagers, whether serf or free, worked the soil according to a system embedded in tradition and sanctioned by custom that had the force of law.

The lord of the manor was around somewhere, and he normally had certain rights to the labor of the villagers and to the product of the land. He also held rights to a set of customary payments. But these rights were always limited, and they did not include the right to organize agricultural production as he saw fit. He could, of course, violate custom (since the peasants had little protection from higher authority), but they might rebel, or they might simply run away and go to colonize eastern Germany or ask for the protection of another lord. The point here is that the lord of the manor did not *own* the land. He was not free to use the property as he saw fit. All he owned was a set of specific customary rights.

When a feudal *seigneur* went east as a Crusader and seized land on Cyprus or elsewhere, he found that these restrictions no longer applied. As a conqueror, he was above the local customary law. He also found another source of authority for the free disposition or management of his land. Slavery survived in the Mediterranean basin, as it had not done north of the Alps. Italy, southern France, and the Iberian Peninsula all had a class of slaves, not serfs, from Roman times down to the sixteenth century, and even later in some cases. Both the Christians and Muslims, furthermore, enslaved their war prisoners when fighting one another.

It was therefore easier here than it was in northern Europe for the lord over conquered land to plan production. Most agricultural workers on Cyprus were local and semiservile, but they were not slaves. The lord could, however, buy imported slaves to supply additional labor, and the new labor force had no rights against the lord in law or custom. He could put them to work at anything he wanted them to do. The feudal *seigneur* thus had the option of becoming something like a capitalist plantation owner in his relationship to agricultural enterprise, though he might remain a feudal *seigneur* in his relations with other members of the upper class.

This entering wedge of agricultural management on a capitalist basis was reinforced from another source. The Italian trading cities had been one of the chief centers for the development of urban, bourgeois attitudes and practices. They were also involved in transporting Crusaders and their supplies. In return, they got feudal land grants in the conquered territory. As a result, Italian city-states rewarded some bourgeois, nonnoble families with fiefs held on feudal tenure. Because these bourgeois tenants had originally been businessmen, accustomed to rational calculation and planning to use their property for the sake of profit, they were not inclined to let the new estates run themselves, as they had been in the past. Instead, they began to apply their commercial managerial habits to agriculture. As time passed, some of their attitudes were transmitted to their new neighbors of feudal origin. Indeed, their children intermarried, and the new rulers of feudal and bourgeois origin blended into a single new class of overlords.

On Cyprus, the ruling Lusignan family was drawn from the French feudal nobility. They came, therefore, from a social setting where trade and commerce were held to be especially demeaning. Once they had risen to become kings of Cyprus, however, they could afford to lower themselves socially in order to manage sugar plantations in a thoroughly capitalist manner, though they retained feudal forms for their relations within the ruling class – for example, by letting out lands on feudal tenure. But the tenants were inhabitants of the Mediterranean basin. One of the great families was the Cornaros from Venice. Another sugar family was

the Ferrer family from Catalonia. Other sugar plantations belonged to the church, and especially to the order of the Hos-
pitalers.

The Cornaro family history shows the route some bourgeois
could take to rise into the nobility. They were originally Venetian
merchants. In 1366, one member of the family received a grant on
feudal tenure from the king of Cyprus, and he began working his
territory in a thoroughly capitalist manner. He bought slaves from
Arabia and Syria and added these to the initial work force of serfs
and refugees from Palestine. The Cornaros irrigated their land
with an expensive system of canals, which also brought water for
the waterwheel they used to crush the cane. They sent to Europe
for copper kettles and other equipment for boiling off the sugar.
They built a full-scale refinery, producing both granulated sugar
and semirefined loaves – rather than just the semirefined product
usually shipped to Europe for later refining. In time, the Cornaros
became the social equals of the Lusignan family, and the two
families intermarried. In the end, it was Catherine Cornaro, the
widow of the last of the house of Lusignan, who presented Cyprus
to the Venetian state in 1489.

Long before that time, the sugar industry had spread widely
throughout the island. The Lusignans, and others who held feudal
grants from them, rented out smaller tracts to a variety of
commercial firms and individuals, especially in the fourteenth
and fifteenth centuries, when the industry was fully established.
In this way it became international, drawing capital and management from many of the Christian states bordering the Mediterranean. Venetians were among the most important, but the Banco
di San Giorgio, the state bank of Genoa, also made important
investments.

The Mediterranean slave trade

These plantations in the eastern Mediterranean were closely
linked to the existing network of the Mediterranean slave trade.
Their owners' position was like that of later firms seeking to
innovate. They had to bring together the factors of production in
new ways – supplying labor and capital to the land they hoped to
develop. Because sugar was a labor-intensive crop, and because

still more labor was required to run the mill, the necessary workers were not likely to be found locally, where all available people were already needed in food production. This meant that the planters had to find immigrants from somewhere else. The problem was not unlike the problem of labor mobility in any other sector of the economy – in new mining operations, for example. In the Mediterranean, the ordinary source of mobile labor for any new industry was the slave trade.

The Belgian historian Charles Verlinden, more than anyone else, is responsible for our revived understanding of medieval Mediterranean slavery and the slave trade. Slavery remained at least a minor aspect of economic life throughout the Mediterranean world until the eighteenth century, long after it had disappeared north of the Alps. Into the seventeenth century and even later, slaves rowed the galleys that were the principal war vessels. Some, especially young boys and young girls, went to harems or for use as prostitutes. Slaves were often used as domestic servants, but they were rarely manual workers in agriculture in either Muslim or Christian Mediterranean countries. Slaves had served as agricultural workers on the Roman latifundia, but the reintroduction of slavery to agriculture was an innovation of the sugar industry.

The source of slaves was varied. Both Christians and Muslims enslaved war captives or the crews and passengers of ships captured at sea – though often for the sake of ransom, rather than labor. Up to about 1204, when Latin Christians captured Constantinople, most of the Mediterranean slave traffic originated in the Mediterranean basin – usually war captives from the land fighting of the Christian reconquest in Spain, or from fighting in Palestine, where the Crusades made warfare a chronic state of affairs.

Once Constantinople was in Western hands, however, Venice and Genoa were able to trade freely past that city. Both set up a series of trading posts on the northern and eastern coasts of the Black Sea. The slave trade flourished there, especially during the early thirteenth century. From 1204 to 1266, when the Latin empire of Constantinople came apart, the Black Sea ports furnished most of the slaves sold in the Mediterranean basin.

Though diminished, this slave trade went on into the fourteenth century. By that time, slaves came from various sources. Some were Tatars from the regions just north of the Black Sea coasts. Others were Mongols drawn from farther east, and a fair number were Russians or Ukrainians from the north. It is hard to estimate the size of this trade – perhaps 1,000 a year would be generous. It was certainly not on the order of 10,000 a year. Only a minority of those who entered the trade would have found their way to the plantations.

This trade made no distinction in terms of race, color, or religion. Christians, in principle, were not supposed to enslave other Christians, but they sometimes did so anyway. A considerable, if minor, undercurrent of trade ran from Greece to Spain. Another ran from Russia into the Roman Catholic world on the excuse that Orthodox Christians were close to being heretics. Bulgarians, Bosnians, and others from the Orthodox world ended in the West as slaves. Thus, the first plantation slaves were neither blacks nor Africans of any color. In fact, this early slave trade had nothing to do with sub-Saharan Africa.

Then, beginning about the middle of the fourteenth century, Africans began to appear in Mediterranean slave markets. They came across the Sahara, first into the Muslim slave markets of North Africa and then by sale into the Christian trade, occasionally by capture in the North African wars. Gradually, a scattering of black Africans found their way into the general pattern of the Mediterranean slave trade. Some came from eastern Africa, north along the Nile Valley. Others came from the central Sudan, north from the region of Lake Chad to present-day Tunisia or Libya. Still others, though fewer, came from the western Sudan across the Sahara to Algeria or Morocco. The trade was so important that the Africans living in Barcelona in the early fifteenth century formed an association of Christian black freedmen – before the Europeans had pushed down the coast of Africa to make maritime contact with the sub-Saharan coasts. Black Africans, however, played only a small part in the broader patterns of Mediterranean slavery before the middle of the fifteenth century.

Two nearly simultaneous events were to change that situation. The Turks captured Constantinople in 1453, which made it much more difficult for Christian ships to reach the slave ports north of the Black Sea. At about the same time, the Portuguese voyagers down the coast of Africa made effective contact with sub-Saharan ports. The Portuguese were then able to tap the sources of the slave trade that had previously flowed north across the Sahara. For the next century, Lagos and Lisbon in Portugal replaced the Black Sea ports as the main centers of supply for the Mediterranean slave trade. With an Atlantic source of labor, it soon became economical to move the plantations closer to the labor supply, and the plantation complex began its first move toward the fuller development of these early institutions.

The mature plantation complex

A search for institutional origins necessarily begins with early and incomplete examples of what was to be. But such a search raises a further question: What was the full-blown plantation complex like? It might be defined by some quantitative measure – demographic, such as the proportion of slaves to the total population; or economic, such as specialized in production for sale at a distance.[3] Or a historian could choose a particular plantation society and look to the past for its origins; for example, an American historian could look for the origins of the southern "Cotton Kingdom" as it existed from about 1830 to 1860. Or a mixed approach could limit the field of choice to preindustrial examples and search for the societies with the most specialized production and the most intense slave regime. By that standard the historical model would be Jamaica, Barbados, or Saint Dominigue (now Haiti) in the eighteenth century – with Brazil in the seventeenth or Mauritius in the early nineteenth as close competitors.

These places, and others that were similar, had a number of features that marked them off from other societies, and especially from contemporaneous Europe, their political master. First, most of the productive labor was forced labor; most people were slaves. This was so in Russia, since serfs were slaves for all practical purposes, but Russian estates were not nearly as specialized as

---

[3]See, for example, Lloyd Best, "A Model of a Pure Plantation Economy," *Social and Economic Studies*, 17:283–326 (1968).

tropical plantations.[4] Nor did preindustrial, non-Western, slave-holding societies in the Muslim world or Southeast Asia have such a high proportion of slaves in the labor force.

Second, the population was not self-sustaining. Neither the European managerial staff nor the African work force produced an excess of births over deaths. Both groups had to be sustained by a constant stream of new population just to maintain their numbers – still more if the system were to grow. Given the present state of demographic information, it is uncertain how widespread this excess of deaths over births was in the American tropics; but it was undoubted in the key islands and colonies of the plantation complex, and it lasted for a long time – at least a century and a half to two centuries and perhaps more. It goes without saying that such a long-term demographic imbalance is unusual. Cities are the only common example of non-self-sustaining populations that kept up their numbers through immigration.[5] Many populations have declined in number – even disappeared altogether – but in the plantation complex at its height, this continuous stream of immigrants not only offset net natural decrease, it tended to grow through time.

Third, agricultural enterprise was organized in large-scale capitalist plantations. Typically, these plantations had fifty to several hundred workers – a far larger scale than that of European agriculture of the time. The owner of the land and the capital equipment managed all steps of production through his agents. On the plantation itself, he gave orders for the conduct of all agricultural operations on a day-to-day and hour-to-hour basis. This again was different from the patterns of work organization and management anywhere in European agriculture.

Fourth, though capitalist, the plantations also had certain features that can be called feudal. Specifically, the owner not only controlled his work force during their working hours, he also had,

---

[4]For a comparison of Russia with the plantation complex, see Peter Kolchin, *Unfree Labor: American Slavery and Russian Serfdom* (Cambridge: Harvard University Press, 1987); Richard Hellie, *Slavery in Russia,1450–1725* (Chicago: Chicago University Press, 1982).
[5]Williams H. McNeil, "Human Migration: A Historical Overview," in W. H. McNeil and Ruth S. Adams (eds.), *Human Migration: Patterns and Policies* (Bloomington: Indiana University Press, 1978), pp. 3–19, has shown that a similar pattern of high net natural decrease fed by continuous immigration was true of many, if not most, cities until recent times.

at least de facto, some form of legal jurisdiction. His agents acted informally as policemen. They punished most minor criminals and settled most disputes without reference to higher authority.

Fifth, the plantations were created to supply a distant market with a highly specialized product, at first mainly sugar but later others, like coffee or cotton. The plantation often grew food to feed its own workers, but at times virtually the whole production was exported. This meant that the society was dependent on long-distance trade to carry off the crop and to bring in supplies, people, and food. When this happened, more of its total consumption and production was carried by long-distance traders than in any other part of the world economy of the time. The possible exceptions were specialized island producers in Asia, like the Maluku islands that supplied Europe and most of Asia with cloves. Certainly no sections of the European or African economies were so intensely export oriented.

Sixth, political control over the system lay on another continent and in another kind of society. Domination from a distance had occurred often enough in history, but rarely from this great a distance. And political control was fragmented. At various times, Portugal, Spain, Holland, England, France, Brandenburg, Sweden, Denmark, and Kurland (more recently Latvia) had a piece of the action. This meant that each overseas part of the system in Africa or the Americas was linked to a metropolis in Europe, and all the European metropolises were linked together through the competitive mechanisms of the European state system.

The list could go on, but these six characteristics seem to be those that set off the tropical Atlantic plantations most clearly from other contemporaneous societies. We can now go back in time to see where they came from – to see, if possible, what historical conditions created and then sustained a politicoeconomic order that appears, on its face, so utterly wasteful and irrational.

Forms of cultural encounter

The peculiarity of the plantation complex stands out clearly in contrast to other forms of cultural encounter between Europe and non-Western societies. In these same centuries, from the sixteenth to the nineteenth, four different balances of cultural demography can be distinguished.

One was the trade diaspora of merchants scattered along trade routes to facilitate trade between people of their own society and their hosts. It was the most ancient form, occurring at all periods back to the Agricultural Revolution. The merchants were nearly always a small minority in the host society, but their need to trade forced them to learn about the local culture – to become, in effect, cross-cultural brokers. The men and women of these trade diasporas therefore enjoyed a cross-cultural experience of unusual intensity.

With the Maritime Revolution of the fifteenth century, Europeans gained the capacity to make direct voyages to virtually any part of the world, and the character of trade diasporas under European control began to change. Some voyages were peaceful and purely commercial in intent and conduct, but by the sixteenth century, most European trade to Asia was militarized, with armed shipping based on fortified trading posts or trading cities like Goa, Bombay, or Batavia. These "trading post empires" were to serve in the longer run as a point of departure for the European conquest of India and Southeast Asia. Meanwhile, they served as a link between Asia and the plantation complex.

A second form of cultural encounter was outright military conquest and rule over an alien society. The Christian West had expanded its control in the Mediterranean basin during the Middle Ages, but Europeans began their imperialist phase overseas with the conquest of highland South and Middle America in the mid-sixteenth century. As the Spanish government took over political power from the Inca and Aztec oligarchies, it needed Spanish cadres as soldiers and officials. A few more Spaniards drifted in as merchants, miners, and sometimes ranchers, but without displacing the native American community. The result was a cultural-demographic type sometimes called "territorial empire" or "true empire." Unlike the trading post empires, where Europeans settled only in crucial strong points, with territorial empires they meant to govern the whole, though with Indian help. The number of Europeans required to run a true empire overseas rarely amounted to as much as 5 percent of the total population. The local communities remained intact and kept much of their culture, even after centuries of European rule.

The earliest examples of true empire were the viceroyalties of New Spain and Peru. By the beginning of the nineteenth century, British India and the Dutch rule over Java had been added, and they expanded during that century to include all of South Asia and Indonesia. After the 1880s, mainland Southeast Asia and sub-Saharan Africa were added. These new European empires outside the Americas, however, came into existence as the plantation complex was being phased out. The empires important to the plantation complex at its height were the nearby empires on the mainland of tropical America.

A third cultural-demographic type is sometimes called "settlement empire" or "true colonization." As Europeans began to settle the North American mainland in the early seventeenth century, they found the native inhabitants to be comparatively few. Many died from their encounter with European diseases. Others were pushed aside or herded into cultural enclaves like the later Indian reservations. This encounter with blanket immigration is in one sense the opposite of true empire. With true empire the natives were many and the alien rulers were few; with true colonization, the natives were few and the alient immigrants were many. The United States is the obvious type case, but Argentina and Uruguay, Australia and New Zealand, and much of Siberia were all added to this category by the nineteenth century.

The fourth major type was the plantation complex, where Europeans conquered and then replaced the vanishing native peoples with settlers – but not settlers from Europe. At first, these settlers were drawn mainly from Africa, but later they came from Asian lands as well.

Both true empire and true colony are demographic extremes, with a wide range of possibilities in between. Where the minority – whether natives or settlers – was at least 5 percent of the total population, it could usually maintain its existence as a community and practice its culture.

Instances where two or more cultural communities exist within a single society are often called "plural societies." European settlers created plural societies in several parts of Africa and Asia – in Africa, Algeria, Tunisia, Zimbabwe, and South Africa; and in

Asia, Israel, and several regions within the USSR. Plural societies in the Americas had a different origin. Until the sixteenth century, the Americas had been isolated from the main disease environments of the Afro-Eurasian landmass. This meant that the native Americans lacked appropriate immunities against the diseases introduced by Europeans and Africans. A series of epidemics reduced most New World populations by as much as 90 percent during the first century and a half after contact. The number of European settlers in South and Middle America was tiny compared to what was to follow in the nineteenth century, but they increased through natural growth, whereas the Indian population diminished. By the late seventeenth century, Mexico and Peru had become plural societies, with Indian and Spanish cultural communities living side by side in the same state. In time, these separate cultural communities influenced each other and created a new, integrated culture as a middle ground between them. In Mexico by the early twentieth century, cultural integration had gone so far that the majority of the people could only be called Mexican, though separate Spanish and Indian cultural communities still existed alongside it.

Still another mixed type came into existense on the North American mainland. Some plantations, especially for tobacco, had begun in the seventeenth century, but the workers were mainly from Europe. In the eighteenth century, however, the slave trade reached North America as well. Throughout the U.S. South, a plantation society grew up alongside the true colony to become a mixed neighbor to the mature plantation societies of the Caribbean.

Suggestions for futher reading

Galloway, J. H. "The Mediterranean Sugar Industry," *Geographical Review*, 67:177–92 (1977).

Mintz, Sydney W., *Sweetness and Power: The Place of Sugar in Modern History* (New York: Viking Press, 1985).

Phillips, William D., Jr., *Slavery from Roman Times to the Early Transatlantic Trade* (Minneapolis: University of Minnesota Press, 1985).

Verlinden, Charles, *The Beginnings of Modern Colonization* (Ithaca: Cornell University Press, 1970).

2

Sugar planting: from Cyprus to the Atlantic islands

As the plantation complex moved out of the Mediterranean, bound for the Caribbean, it changed. First of all, the scale of operations in the Mediterranean was small, and the relative weight of the complex in the Mediterranean economy was also small. In addition, the Mediterranean slave trade of the Middle Ages mainly supplied service slaves destined to be soldiers, domestic servants, concubines, harem guards, and the like – occupations of particular trust or intimacy that were better done by strangers than by people from within the Mediterranean society. The Mediterranean slave trade supplied a few plantation workers as well, but the Atlantic slave trade dealt mainly in agricultural labor. On Mediterranean plantations, many workers were slaves, but not all. In the later plantations at the height of the system, all were slaves. Indeed, most of the drivers and foremen in the sugar house – definitely management, even at a low level – were slaves as well.

The demography of the Mediterranean and Atlantic slave trades also appears to have been different. Deaths exceeded births on the West Indian plantations from the sixteenth century on, and the slave trade supplied the deficit. The migration of the slaves was not, therefore, a one-time event. The plantations needed a continuous supply of a new labor, if only to remain the same size. Growth required still more. We know less about the demography of Mediterranean slavery, but from what is known about the epidemiology and environment, after the first generation a net natural decrease in plantation populations would not be expected. First-generation losses were the rule, because the Mediterranean

17

slavers sold more women into service slavery and more men to the plantations. After the first generation, the number of men and women would have been more nearly equal.

The Atlantic islands

Sugar grows best where heat and water are plentiful all year round. The Mediterranean is therefore less than ideal. Even the southern Mediterranean has a cool season in the winter and a dry season in the summer. With the European maritime revolution beginning in the fifteenth century, Europeans had easy access to the Atlantic islands, and some of them had a far better environment for sugar cultivation.

The climate of these islands varied enormously – from the Mediterranean type of southern Europe, to semidesert, to wet tropics. The Azores, for example, lay far out in the Atlantic due west of Portugal, with a climate much like that of mainland Portugal. They were uninhabited when Europeans first discovered them between 1427 and 1431. European settlers from Portugal followed during the next century, growing crops they had grown on the mainland – wheat, wine, and olives, not tropical staples like sugar. The Azores were therefore true colonies, not plantation colonies. They were to be stepping stones to later colonization of the New World, but not for the plantation complex. Their chief importance for the plantation complex was strategic, covering the return from the New World to Europe by way of the belt of prevailing westerly winds.

Farther to the south was Madeira, or the Madeiras, two habitable islands and a number of smaller islets. The largest, Madeira proper, was about thirty-four miles long by fourteen miles wide. The other island, Porto Santo, was tiny by comparison. Yet this insignificant island group became, for a time, the key center of European sugar production – and the crucial stepping stone to carry the plantation regime from the Mediterranean to the New World. When Europeans first visited, perhaps in the fourteenth century, Madeira was completely uninhabited. It lay off the coast of Morocco in a similar climatic zone, but with a bit more rainfall because of its maritime setting and volcanic peaks. The final Portuguese exploration and settlement came after about 1420, coinciding with the maritime push down the African coast.

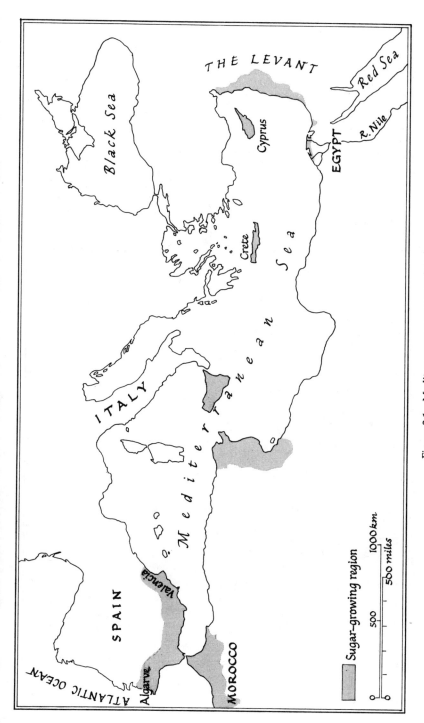

Figure 2.1 Mediterranean sugar growing.

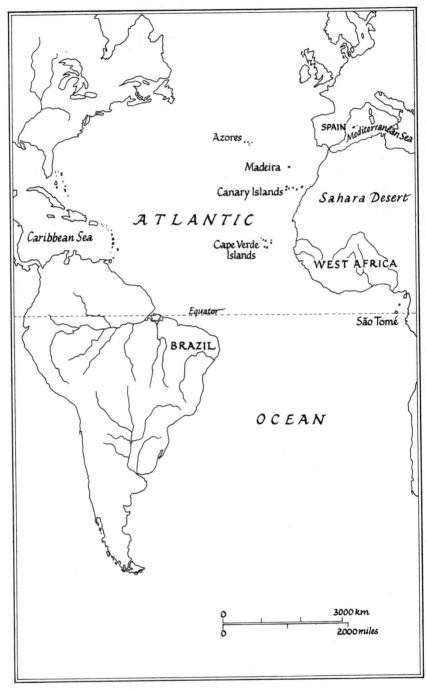

Figure 2.2 Tropical Atlantic.

About 250 miles due south and closer to the African coast lay the Canary Islands, which also played a role in the westward movement of the sugar economy. Like Maderia, the Canaries were volcanic islands, but higher, more rugged, with less flat land suitable for sugar. They were also drier, with less certainty of good rainfall. Sugar cultivation was possible, but conditions were far from ideal. The islands had been known to the Romans, but Europeans lost track of them during the Middle Ages, though Moroccans apparently visited from time to time. In the early fourteenth century, Western mariners rediscovered the islands – first the Portuguese, later the Spanish. For a time in the fourteenth century their control was hotly contested by the two Hispanic powers, but the Spanish finally made good their claim and the islands remained Spanish after 1480.

Still farther south, the Cape Verde Islands represent a further step in aridity. They lie straight west of the mouth of the Senegal River, at nearly the same latitude as the sahel that separates the Sahara desert from the savanna country of West Africa. The climate is much the same as that of coastal Senegal – ideal for tourism but far too dry for reliable sugarcane productions. The islands were uninhabited, though when the Portuguese first discovered them in the late fifteenth century, and they made a convenient offshore base for trade with western Africa.

A final group of four islands lay still farther south, around the bulge of Africa in the Gulf of Guinea – São Tomé, Fernando Po, Principe, and Annobon. Europeans discovered all four of these volcanic peaks in 1471 and 1472, and the Portuguese crown claimed them a little later. Only Fernando Po and São Tomé, however, were important in the sixteenth century. Fernando Po had an existing African population, but São Tomé was uninhabited and provided a clean slate for a new sugar industry.

Thus, of the five island groups, the Gulf of Guinea islands were best for sugar but far from Europe. Madeira and the Canaries could support plantations, but they could also serve as true colonies with a European population – and in the long run that is what they became, after a plantation phase had come and gone. The Azores were ideal for true colonies, and the Cape Verdes were useful only as a base of trade with nearby Africa.

The whole set of island groups had a special attraction for

Europeans in the fifteenth and sixteenth centuries. Europeans overseas were comparatively few, and whatever military strength they had depended on their maritime ability. Islands were safer and more easily dominated than equivalent spots on the mainland. Only Fernando Po and the Canaries had a native population, and the Canary Islanders died off rapidly on contact with European diseases. The Europeans were free to take over the land; all they needed was people to work it.

Colonial institutions: the Canaries

As European colonization moved out into the Atlantic, the patterns of political and social control moved as well and changed in the process. The Atlantic islands in the fifteenth century thus came to be an intermediate step between the colonial institutions of the medieval Mediterranean and those of the Americas.

The Canary Islands, discovered in the 1320s – a full century before the major Portuguese explorations farther south – are a useful illustration. The native peoples were relatives of the Berbers of the nearby North African mainland. At the time of discovery, they had been cut off so long from the mainland that they were still in the Neolithic Age, lacking even the knowledge of metal working, which by that time had spread to the entire continent of Africa. Their isolation meant that they also lacked immunities from important European diseases. They began to die on their first contact with the Europeans, and they are now extinct.

Typical of many Atlantic voyages at this time and later, the sponsor was royal – King Denis of Portugal – but the personnel were Italians serving under Manuel Pessagno, who had been grand marshall of Genoa. Again typical of the times, Pessagno received a normal feudal charter over any lands he might discover, as well as some feudal grants in Portugal itself – presumably to cover his expenses in case he discovered nothing at all. Pessagno, in turn, recruited some twenty captains of galleys in Genoa. One of these captains discovered the Canary Islands between 1325 and 1339. The Portuguese began to establish settlements shortly afterward, but they were later driven away by superior Spanish power, and the islands became Spain's main stepping stone to the New World.

It is hardly surprising that a conquest this early in time followed medieval forms. It was, after all, contemporaneous with the last phases of the reconquest of peninsular Iberia and even a little earlier than the most active Genoese colonial efforts in the eastern Mediterranean. The legal forms were patterned exactly on those of the reconquest in Portugal. The military forms were patterned on those of the Genoese in the Levant at this same period – as might be expected, since the concessionaires were Italian.

Nor were the men who undertook the conquest and settlement feudal lords. They were merchants, ship masters, and capitalists, but happy enough to hold feudal concessions, if only to exploit them in their own capitalist way. Some of the later concessionaires were companies rather than individuals. Their apparent first intent was to set up something like the European manorial system, even though they themselves had no intention of settling down to enjoy their dominance over the countryside. They could hardly have envisaged, at this stage, the plantation regime that was to come, much less the ships of the trading post empires that were to pass on their way to the Indian Ocean or the cargoes of African slaves that would someday flow past them on the way north.

The capitalist element in this mixture of capitalism and feudalism was to become clearer a century or so later, when Europeans reached Madeira and the Gulf-of-Guinea islands. By the time explorers reached São Tomé, the possiblity of using slaves from Africa on sugar estates was well known, though the legal titles were set in feudal forms. In 1500, the crown gave a certain Fernão de Mello a feudal grant to control São Tomé, and he proceeded to establish sugar plantations worked by African slaves.

The westward migration

São Tomé was the last of the Atlantic islands to be developed – the end product of the line of westward migration by sugar planta-tions that stretched back to the Levant, if not to India. The driving force was partly the expanding European demand for sugar, partly the technological change in sugar crushing, which made larger land holding units desirable, and partly the rise of Genoa in the Mediterranean, which shifted the emphasis from the eastern to the western basin. New sources of capital were also available in Genoa itself, but also in southern Germany, where the trans-Alpine trade had prospered during the fifteenth century. In the 1460s and later, the Grosse Ravensburger Gesellschaft held extensive sugar estates near both Valencia and Malaga in southern Spain. The main agents, however, were the Genoese, whose long-standing contacts with Sicily made it easy for them to pass on the technology, first to southern Iberia and then out into the Atlantic.

Madeira was crucial; it was Portuguese and the natural stepping stone on the way to Brazil. Sugar planting came in 1455, thirty-five years after the place had first been settled. At that time, growing cane and processing it were still separate operations. Mills, with their large capital investment, were crucial, but most of the cane was grown by small cane farmers who sold to the mill. The capital was largely Genoese, though some was Portuguese. Technicians came from Sicily. In most ways, the move was typical of earlier westward steps of the Mediterranean plantation complex.

Economically, it was different. Madeira was out in the Atlantic, far from Genoa or Leghorn but relatively close to Antwerp, and direct shipping to Antwerp began in 1472. By 1480, Antwerp had seventy ships in the sugar trade of Madeira alone. Production rose from seventy-two metric tons in 1455 to 760 metric tons in 1493 – and to 2,400 metric tons by 1570. Refineries and distribution networks for northern Europe were also based at Antwerp. By 1500 Madeira sugar dominated the northern European market, and it also sold in Genoa and even in Istanbul on the doorstep of earlier production centers in the Levant and Cyprus. The Canaries were a Spanish equivalent of Madeira, with Genoese enterprise and German capital, as in southern Spain itself.

The movement to São Tomé was a longer step. Here was an island off the coast of Africa far from Europe, but it had the advantages of a tropical climate, rich volcanic soils, and nearby sources of labor from the kingdoms of Kongo and Benin. Sugar production began to rise a little after 1500, reaching 2,250 metric tons by 1544 (nearly the same as that of Madeira), but that was the peak. The defense of the island became very expensive as Angolan slaves escaped into the mountains, set up a free African community, and raided sugar plantations. The Portuguese were notwilling to invest heavily in the military defense of such a far-off place. Over the next decades, these raids, plus competition from still newer plantations in Brazil, drove the São Tomé sugar estates out of the market. The rebel slaves, moreover, were not conquered for another 300 years.

To the Americas

Once on the Atlantic islands, it was a small matter to carry the sugar industry across the ocean to the American colonies. But this further movement brought some changes. In the Mediterranean, the sugar industry had been international. Investment had come from all over Europe; individual estate owners were an international group who worked under various feudal or national authorities. Italian influence was strong, though political control was Spanish or Portuguese.

With the movement across the Atlantic, the sugar industry split into national sections – each jealously guarded from foreign influence, as Spain and Portugal both tried as much as possible to keep colonial shipping as a national monopoly. The northern European web of international commercial contacts weakened, though Flemish capital remained important in Brazil, as it had been in Madeira. The Hispanic powers in transatlantic trade adopted the militant relations that had characterized the Venetian–Genoese trade wars in the Mediterranean. The change reflected the rise of the national monarchies and the fact that Spain or Spain and Portugal together were at war with some combination of the Dutch, English, and French throughout the last third of the sixteenth century and into the seventeenth.

By the 1490s, Spain had its Atlantic extension to the Canaries. The Portuguese had theirs to Madeira. At the next stage, when the Portuguese moved on down the African coast to São Tomé, the Spanish sugar industry began to move on to the island of Hispaniola or Santo Domingo in the Caribbean. Columbus introduced sugarcane on his second voyage in 1493. Nothing came of it, and Columbus himself was still intent on the possibility of a trading post empire off the coast of Asia, where he still supposed Santo Domingo to be. In 1503, the Spanish reintroduced sugarcane with Canary Island technicians. This time, it failed for lack of labor. The local Arawak Indians had already begun to die off on contact with European diseases. In 1517, the Spanish tried again with men and machines from the Canaries. This time, it succeeded for a while, and sugar production rose steadily until it reached about 1,000 metric tons a little before 1570.

Then expansion stopped. A few new sugar plantations appeared in Jamaica, Puerto Rico, and coastal Mexico, but the essential problems remained. The demographic disaster in the tropical lowlands meant that the local sources of forced labor dried up. Portugal, not Spain, had the contacts on the African coast that would have made Africa a viable source. The Spanish government had more serious concerns in highland Peru and Mexico, with their well-publicized supplies of gold and silver. Neither Hispaniola nor São Tomé was to amount to much after the mid-sixteenth century.

Brazil was another matter, and it had several advantages. The voyage from Africa to Brazil took less than half the time of a voyage from Africa to the Caribbean. Portugal dominated – virtually monopolized – the Atlantic slave trade well into the seventeenth century, and, lacking the distraction of Peru and Mexico, the Portuguese were willing to put more resources into sugar planting. Yet in the much longer run, the western end of the island of Hispaniola was destined to become the French colony of Saint Domingue, the most prized of all sugar colonies in the eighteenth century.

The Portuguese success is clear enough from production and export figures, even allowing a wide margin for error. The Portuguese introduced sugar from Madeira to Brazil only in the mid-1540s. By 1560, production had reached about 2,500 metric tons (roughly the production of either Madeira or São Tomé at that time). By 1580, it had doubled once more to reach 5,000 tons. By 1600, it was up to 16,000 tons, and, by 1630, it was more than 20,000 tons. There it stabilized, between 20,000 and 30,000 tons a year during the rest of the seventeenth century. By the mid-seventeenth century, in short, Brazil had reached about ten times the production of the richest sugar colonies elsewhere, whereas the Caribbean as a whole hardly produced one-tenth as much sugar as Brazil.

These numbers are important, not for their own sake but because they help to put a brake on our normal expectations. Because Santo Domingo and Cuba later became big sugar centers, we half expect them to have been big at the beginning. Because São Tomé never developed, we – and most writers on Latin American history – forget that it ever rivaled the economic importance of Brazil.

Why migration?

Sixteenth-century navigation made it possible to reach the Americas or India, but only at great cost and with heavy losses in ships and men. To set up agricultural operations 3,000 to 6,000 miles from the market seems improbable, especially when sugar making called for such heavy capital expenditure and slave labor cost still more. Yet people did it and apparently it was profitable, at least for some.

The growth of wealth, and hence of sugar consumption in northern Europe, is part of the explanation. Once shipping had improved enough to carry sugar at a salable price from Madeira to Portugal or Genoa, the cost of sea transport to Antwerp was very little greater. Map distances are deceptive. In most seasons, Madeira was downwind from Gibraltar. Instead of tracking upwind against northeast trades and a current from the northeast as well, a ship bound for Europe sailed northwest on a long tack as close as possible to the trade wind, until it reached the vicinity of the Azores. Once there, prevailing westerlies made for an easy return to Portugal or the Mediterranean – but the voyage to the English Channel was no more difficult. The actual sailing time from Madeira to Genoa or from Madeira to Antwerp was much the same.

Northern Europe was also growing faster economically than southern Europe in the late sixteenth century. Because sugar was still too expensive for mass consumption, wealth or concentrations of wealth made a real difference in economic demand. Shipping technology also improved steadily during the sixteenth century and on into the seventeenth, and the Low Countries were the leaders of Europe in carrying bulk cargoes. The Flemish had a long-standing interest in the Madeira sugar and an incentive to take a more active role in Brazil as well.

The migration of the sugar industry also gained something from what economists call the "clean-slate advantage." When the industry was first established in a particular place, the size of the mill controlled the amount of cane land needed to supply it. Once the investment was placed, mill size and landholding units were hard to change. Yet a few decades later, new investors on new land, using the best technology available in *their* time, had a decided advantage. Old plantations also lost out because nutrients in the soil were not replaced by adequate fertilizers.

Some of sugar's stepping stones between the Levant and the Caribbean were logical and convenient for that time and place, but these areas no longer grew sugar cane. This was true of the Mediterranean generally. It is also true of some Caribbean islands that once produced very little but sugar – Grenada, St. Lucia, and Nevis, for example. On Madeira, sugarcane still grew on a small scale up to the recent past, but only with heavy tariff protection. Wine has long since replaced sugar as the principal export. Both São Tomé and the Canaries have stopped producing sugar, though parts of northeast Brazil still produce cane sugar in the final quarter of the twentieth century.

Suggestions for further reading

Canny, Nicholas, and Anthony Pagden, *Colonial Identity in the Atlantic World, 1500–1800* (Princeton: Princeton University Press, 1987).

Davis, Ralph, *The Rise of the Atlantic Economies* (Ithaca: Cornell University Press, 1973).

Duncan, T. Bentley, *Atlantic Islands: Madeira, the Azores and the Cape Verdes in the Seventeenth-Century Commerce and Navigation*(Chicago: University of Chicago Press, 1972).

Fernández-Armesto, Felipe, *Before Columbus: Exploration and Colonization from the Mediterranean to the Atlantic, 1229–1492* (Philadelphia: University of Pennsylvania Press, 1987).

Parry, J. H., *The Age of Reconnaissance: Discovery, Exploration, and Settlement, 1450–1650* (Cleveland: World Publishing, 1963).

Schwartz, Stuart, *Sugar Plantations in the Formation of Brazilian Society: Bahia, 1550–1835* (Cambridge: Cambridge University Press, 1985).

3

Africa and the slave trade

Africa and African history have a peculiar place in Western historical writing and in Western consciousness. Some of it has to do with the special relationships between Africa and Western civilization over the past 400 or 500 years, and especially with the fact that Africans were the principal slaves in the Western-controlled world from the sixteenth century well into the nineteenth. But that was not always so. The prototypical slaves in the medieval world were Slavs – the people exported from the Black Sea slave trading posts. In classical Latin, the word for "slave" was *manicipium*, but the predominance of Slavic people in the medieval trade added a new term, *sclavus*. This word and its successors, like "slave," have been the dominant terms for people owned by other people in most European languages ever since.

People of African descent were nevertheless the stereotypical slaves in Western societies from the sixteenth century to the nineteenth, and this fact of history was one source of Western suppositions about alleged African racial inferiority. And Africa's exceptional place in Western thought continued well into the twentieth century. Africa was the last of the inhabited continents to have its history included in the curricula of European and American universities.

African isolation

The peculiarity of African–Western relations goes back even further. Sub-Saharan West Africa was close to the Mediterranean world but was comparatively unknown. It had had some contact

29

with the Mediterranean civilizations as far back as the first millennium B.C. – 800 to 1000 B.C. But that contact across the Sahara was neither regular nor systematic. The knowledge of iron smelting crossed from north to south in that first millennium B.C. Knowledge about certain crops first domesticated in tropical Africa – sesame seed, for example – crossed from south to north. But contact was not regular enough to carry with it systematic knowledge. Romans of the empire knew a good deal about the Red Sea, about the fringes of central Asia, about India, and about the East African coast, but they left no recorded knowledge of what went on beyond the Sahara to the west of the Nile Valley.

One way to clarify the long-term relationships between Africa and early civilizations elsewhere is to use the concept of "intercommunicating zones" in world history. Before the Agricultural Revolution, about 10,000 to 5,000 years B.C., when people first began to plant and harvest crops, most people lived in isolated hunting and gathering or fishing societies, each having comparatively little contact with its neighbors. Agriculture made possible an economic surplus over mere subsistence, made possible more specialization, division of labor, and the formation of denser patterns of residence – in time, cities. With cities and trade between them, individual ways of life could change in response to new sources of outside information. Isolated culture areas gave way to intercommunicating zones of more or less homogeneous culture – first in Mesopotamia, then in the Indus Valley of present-day Pakistan, the Nile Valley, and the Yellow River Valley of China. In time, the whole of the Mediterranean basin became part of an intercommunicating zone. By the last centuries B.C., it had regular contact with India, as well as Mesopotamia, and it had distant knowledge of the Chinese empire that was a contemporary of the Roman. Both empires gave political form to intercommunicating zones that were beginning to have a common culture.

At the very earliest stages of the great river valley civilizations like those of Mesopotamia and Egypt, the Sahara desert had been no barrier, but a revolutionary shift in the world's climatic patterns took place about 2500 B.C. In Europe, it was associated with the retreat of the last great glaciers. In Africa, it brought about the desiccation of the belt of land between present-day Mauritania and the Red Sea, creating the Sahara desert. It was only a little earlier than this, about 3200 B.C., that the earliest pharaohs of Egypt had united the Nile Valley below the first cataract, giving political form to the culture that had been taking shape in the previous few hundred years. Gradually after 2500 B.C., Egypt and northwestern Africa became more and more closely related to the net of closer intercommunication of the Mediterranean world. Africa south of the desert, however, lost its contacts with that zone. In the intercommunicating zone, new technology or new discoveries in any part of it were quickly known and taken up wherever they appeared to be useful. Sub-Saharan Africa was largely cut off and went its own way as a series of loosely interconnected societies.

The barrier of the Sahara was not impermeable. The Nile Valley provided one corridor between the Mediterranean and the savanna country south of the desert. The Red Sea was another. The Nilotic Sudan and the Ethiopian highlands were therefore in good contact with the Mediterranean world from Roman times on, but local conditions made it hard to get from these regions to the rest of sub-Saharan Africa. They were, in this sense, semiisolated. Parts of the Nilotic Sudan and the Ethiopian highlands, for example, converted to Christianity shortly after Rome did.

The comparative isolation of the rest of Africa began to break down in a series of stages lasting for over 2,000 years. The first stage was the increasing intensity of long-distance trade in the Red Sea and the Indian Ocean about the second century B.C. By the second century A.D., it was usual for Roman ships (manned by Greek-speaking Egyptians) to sail not only to India but also down the East African coast as far as coastal Tanzania. By the thirteenth century, and probably much earlier, Arab successors of the early Roman mariners had gained control of port towns as far away as Kilwa in southern Tanzania, with further trade contacts south to the Mozambique channel and inland to the gold fields of present-day Zimbabwe.

In West Africa, meanwhile, even the relative isolation began to break down about 500 A.D. with the introduction of camels. These animals had been domesticated in Arabia, and had diffused south into what is now Somalia and then westward along the southern fringes of the Sahara. Desert people, presumed to be the ancestors of the present-day Tuareg, then introduced them into Northwest Africa, the Maghrib in Arabic terminology.

Our knowledge of sub-Saharan West Africa is weak for the period before about 800 A.D., when the rise of Islam made Arabic records available. Archaeological evidence, however, suggests that the southern shore of the desert was already densely populated by people who had a social organization based on kinship ties, but who also had political forms that are properly called states. They also had cities, based mainly on commerce, at least as far south as Jenne in the southern part of present-day Mali, hundreds of miles south of the desert edge.

Trade by camel caravans became a regular feature of life in the western Sahara between about 500 and 800 A.D. Camels are a somewhat paradoxical beast of burden. Their ability to go for long periods without water is well known; so too is the fact that they cannot thrive in very humid climates, or that they can graze on sparse vegetation where rainfall hardly rises above five inches a year. They were also by far the most efficient pack animals known, with relatively high speeds on the road, low maintenance costs, and low costs in human labor per ton mile. Once camels were available, the Sahara not only stopped being a barrier, it became a region of comparatively cheap transportation – an advantage not unlike that of the sea over most forms of land transport. East–west transport in either North Africa or West Africa often used camels that went out into the desert and returned to the sahel, or desert shore, only as they neared their destination. Some authorities have argued that the introduction of camels into North Africa led to a sharp decline in cart transport using the remains of the Roman road system.[1]

The people who pioneered the long-distance trade across the Sahara were from the oases fringing the more arable land in North Africa. These oases were often river valleys, whose streams were underground. They nevertheless made irrigation possible by tapping the flow of water falling on the mountains to the north or west. Otherwise the region was a semidesert, with rainfall in the range of five to twenty inches a year. These conditions were ideal

---

[1] Richard W. Bullet, *The Camel and the Wheel* (Cambridge: Harvard University Press, 1975); W. H. McNeill, "The Eccentricity of Wheels, or Eurasian Transportation in Historical Perspective," *American Historical Review*, 92:1111–26 (1987).

for camel herding. They were also ideal for growing dates. The
date palm is one of the most productive trees known. Under
favorable conditions, a single date palm can produce 100 to 200
pounds of fruit a year, and conditions in these oases were very
favorable. Date palms require irrigation water; rainfall can
actually damage them. But, like sugar, dates were not wanted as
a staple food. Date producers, however, could maximize their
income by trading most of the product to the grain farmers and
textile producers of the North African mountains and coastal
lowlands, using their camel herds for transport. With this
experience, it was a natural step to extend their trade across the
Sahara as well.

Political forms south of the Sahara

Between about 800 and 1200 A.D., partly in response to these new
currents of trade, Africans in the southern sahel developed a set
of trading states with an elaborate organization. Many of the
courts and merchants converted to Islam, so that they soon
became literate in Arabic – in the sense that at least a class of
scribes could read and write. Of these states, the best known, from
west to east, were Takrur in the Senegal Valley, Ghana in the sahel
north of the middle Niger and middle Senegal, Songhai near the
Niger bend, and Kanem near Lake Chad.

Still other states grew up farther south, away from the desert
edge but in contact with desert-oriented trade. One of the most
important was Mali, centered on the upper Niger River and
sometimes ruling territory right to the desert edge. Another set of
city-states appeared in what is now northern Nigeria, where the
Hausa language was and is still spoken. Still others lay to the
south near the boundary between the open savanna and the
tropical forest. Oyo, in present-day western Nigeria, was one of
these, and the nearby kingdom of Benin lay in the forest itself and
had access to the sea through the system of creeks and lagoons
that stretched westward from the Niger delta.

But state formation in tropical Africa was not simply a reflex of
developing external trade. Well before 1500 A.D., a number of
states had come into existence, that had no connection at all with
the trade across the Sahara. Some, like the kingdom of Kongo near

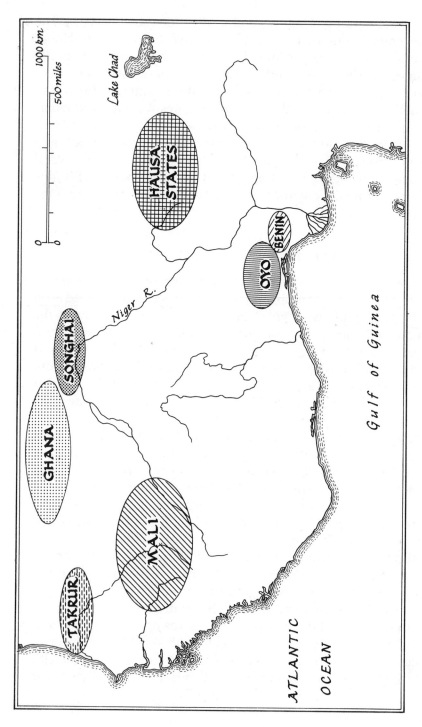

Figure 3.1 Medieval West Africa.

the mouth of the Congo or Zaire River, were in the savanna belt south of the tropical forest – well out of range of trade to the Mediterranean at any period before the Portuguese mariners appeared in the fifteenth century.

But much of sub-Saharan Africa was not organized in states, much less in large empires on the order of Mali. West Africa had many regions of "stateless society," where kinship patterns formed the basis for settling disputes and where no one individual was permanently in charge; no individual, or any small group, held or claimed a monopoly over the right to use force. In the past, some historians thought that these stateless societies were "primitive" or "less developed" forms of government that would naturally give way to the state forms as soon as people found out about state styles of government. More recently, it became clear that a powerful state is not necessarily an advantage for those who live under its control. Stateless societies have therefore persisted alongside states for centuries, apparently by choice. Many of these stateless peoples, for that matter, have had more advanced agricultural techniques than those who lived in states. Historians now believe that statelessness was often preferred, but that states were sometimes essential to meet the threat of foreign military power. States were also useful, though not essential, for the protection of long-distance trade.

The trans-Sahara trade

Long-distance trade was very old in West Africa and the Congo basin alike, certainly older than the developed caravan trade across the desert. Trade tended to emerge wherever climatic differences, like those along the desert fringe, made exchange between cattleherding seminomads and sedentary farmers a good bargain for either side. Farther south, along the fringe between the forest and the savanna, conditions for trade were also favorable. Kola nuts from the forest were a stimulant a little like coffee, and they were widely sold in the savanna country from an early period. Foodstuffs from the forest or savanna also moved back and forth over short distances. Salt was generally in short supply in West Africa, so that most regions had to import it from the coastal salt pans or from rock salt deposits in the desert. Placer

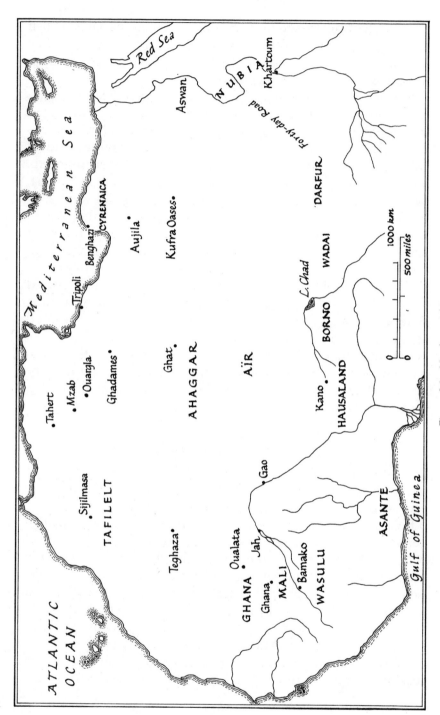

Figure 3.2 Northern Africa.

gold deposits were also worked at several points in West Africa and in time gold became the most important export to the north.

Before the Maritime Revolution brought the Portuguese to the coasts, trade in West Africa and across the desert was carried by a series of interlocked trade diasporas – people of similar ethnic background who settled along the trade routes to facilitate trade by people like themselves. One group of similar diasporas originated in the oases fringing North Africa – places like Sijilmasa in the Ziz Valley of Morocco and the Mzab Valley of southern Algeria, or cities like Ghat and Ghadames in the Fezzan region of central Libya. They had the camels and access to North African or European goods from the north. They carried these goods to one of a series of desert ports on the fringes of arable land to the south – points that were often the capitals of the northern fringe of West African states.

At this point, trade passed over to another set of trade diasporas based south of the Sahara – most often Soninke in culture in the far west, Songhai on the Niger River up or downstream from the northern bend, or Hausa-speaking people south and west of Lake Chad. By the fifteenth century, these desert-edge traders had reached south to the main sources of gold, even to the Akan gold fields in the forests of present-day Ghana. They or other diasporas originating near the forest fringe brought kola nuts for distribution in the savanna and even for sale to North Africa. Still other groups carried goods east and west – like the Mali traders who worked the east–west salt trade from the lower Gambia inland to the Niger Valley. South of the forest, still other trade diasporas carried goods through the savannas south of the Congo basin.

When the European mariners landed on the coasts, they found a network of trade routes that crisscrossed tropical Africa. These routes carried a variety of goods for internal sale – kola nuts, shea butter, several kinds of salt, textiles in varying styles and patterns, iron and iron tools, and some slaves for sale within West Africa. Most African societies made it a practice to enslave war prisoners, but the victors rarely kept these people as servants. If they came from nearby, it was all too easy to escape, perhaps killing some of the captor's people in the process. Many, if not most, war prisoners were therefore sold to passing traders, who took them along the trade routes with their other goods to sell them in distant places where escape would be more difficult.

Traders also carried a variety of goods to the desert edge for export to the north; gold was the most important, but exports included several kinds of pepper, shea butter, some dried meat and hides, and a little ivory. They also carried some slaves for sale in North Africa, but not as the dominant export. Recent estimates put this trade in the range of 500 of 4,000 slaves a year, with a substantial margin for error. When the Europeans appeared on the coast, they found existing trade networks that they could use. They had no need to set up trading posts or to introduce new currents of trade, as they did in dealing with the Ameridians of North America.

Disease and isolation

When they arrived on the African coasts, the Europeans found a situation different from anything they encountered in the Americas or in Asia. The West African disease environment was nearly as dangerous for them as their European diseases were for the American Indians. And it was equally dangerous for the North African traders, who rarely took up residence south of the port cities on the desert edge. From any point of view, tropical West Africa had a terrible disease environment for human beings of any origin. Infection rates with yaws, Guinea worm, trypanosomiasis (sleeping sickness), onchocerciasis (river blindness), and schistosomiasis (liver flukes) were extremely high. In addition, the Africans had the usual range of Old World diseases, such as smallpox, measles, and the common childhood diseases that killed the American Indians. The only diseases that were markedly less serious than they were in Europe were pneumonia and tuberculosis.

What made the environment so dangerous for outsiders, however, was a combination of yellow fever and *Plasmodium falciparum*, the most fatal form of malaria. Africa also had the two most effective inset vectors for malaria found anywhere in the world – *Anopheles gambiae* and *Anopheles funestus*. As a result of these insects, almost the whole of tropical Africa is still considered to be hyperendemic with falciparum malaria, which means, in effect, that the chance of an alien visitor's escaping an infective bite for as long as a year is negligible. Nor is this merely a matter of high humidity in the tropical rain forest. These particular vectors are just as effective in the open savanna country, and they provide some infective bites even during the long dry season.

Falciparum malaria is now found on all continents, but many authorities believe that it originated in West Africa. Whereas the most common species of *plasmodia* found in Europe or in the Americas are mainly debilitating, falciparum malaria is often fatal, especially to children or to adults who are infected for the first time. For nonimmune adults before quinine was available, the case fatality rate varied between about 25 and 75 percent. Children who escaped death still kept the parasite in their bloodstream, but without clinical symptoms as long as they were reinfected with the same strain of *P. falciparum*. Thus, all African children fought a life-and-death battle with the disease. If they survived to the age of five or so, they acquired an apparent immunity – paid for with an infant mortality from malaria alone that would kill half or more of all children before they reached the age of five.

Yellow fever works differently. It is caused by a virus, not a protozoan, like malaria. With yellow fever it is possible to acquire lifelong immunity after an infection, with no clinical symptoms at all. This kind of immunity is common among children who grow up in regions where yellow fever is found. Nonimmune adults who encounter the disease for the first time, however, have a case fatality rate of 75 percent or more, but the survivors acquire lifelong immunity. This pattern of immunity means that the disease appears mainly as an epidemic among nonimmune persons, and it might well disappear but for the fact that the virus parasitizes a number of forest monkeys as well as humans.

For visitors to West Africa who arrived as adults, the combination could be disastrous. A lot depended on the incidence of yellow fever epidemics, but the cost of sending European adults to serve in West Africa was always high. So was the cost to North Africans who crossed the desert, as the French were to find when they sent Algerians to build the Senegal Railway in the late nineteenth century. One survey, based on the personnel records of the Royal African Company between 1695 and 1722, showed that, of every ten men it sent to serve in West Africa, six died in the first year, two died in the second through the seventh years, and only one lived to be discharged in Britain.[2] In the period 1817–36, prequinine years when both Britain and France kept European troops on the West African coast, the range of loss lay between 165 and 430 per thousand. Clearly, this rate was too high to justify a very heavy commitment of Europeans to African campaigns.

African, Muslim, and European slavery

The essence of the slave trade was that people, defined in some way as slaves, were purchased in Africa and sold in the Americas or to North Africa. But the term "slave" creates problems. In common use, it usually means a person over whom another person holds certain rights, which are, in turn, transferable to a third party in return for payment. But this simple matter of salability is not always the most important characteristic of human institutions of social subordination. Serfs on medieval manors in northern Europe were social subordinates, but normally they could only be transferred along with the land they worked. Wives in many socieities had no more rights than slaves, but they were frequently hard to transfer. Many aspects other than the manner of transfer could be far more important – the nature of the work organization, the rights of a subordinate against his master, his chances of manumission, and so on.

The kind of slavery that became dominant in the American plantation was special, different from slavery in most of the Muslim world and different again from slavery in West Africa. The slave was purchased to serve as a unit of labor, normally labor in agricultural work under continuous supervision during the entire work day. In sugar fields, this meant gang work with a driver giving orders hour by hour, if not minute by minute. Tightly disciplined gang work is obviously very different from domestic service, where the slave is a member of the household, however subordinate, and different again from other kinds of agricultural labor where the slave controlled his own activities,

---

[2] K. G. Davies, "The Living and the Dead: White Mortality in West Africa, 1684–1732," in Stanley L. Engerman and Eugene D. Genovese (eds.), *Race and Slavery in the Western Hemisphere: Quantitative Studies* (Princeton: Princeton University Press, 1975), pp. 83–98.

paying the master part of his total income. All three of these forms of work organization existed in American slavery, so that even within the Americas the status of slaves was not the same everywhere.

Slavery in the Muslim world, where African slaves also went, was again different in both theory and practice. There the slave was not a labor unit. The sanction for slavery came from Islam, principally from the belief that pagans were without the law but that they could legitimately be converted by force through enslavement. A slave was thought of as part of the master's household, as a kind of ward undergoing education. His or her status was assimilated to that of a child in the same society, but still as a person – not just a posssession. The master was obliged to undertake his or her religious education, though it rarely reached a very high level. Nor was a slave restricted to hard agricultural labor.

Slaves were subordinate aliens, and Muslim society thought of certain occupations as peculiarly appropriate for them. Most of these were service occupations, often the intimate domestic service of the master such as that of a concubine or harem guard. As strangers, slaves lacked kin or other supporters in the local society. As an owner of strangers, a master might find it useful to have them exercise authority in his own name, even over free people. In the Ottoman Empire, much of the bureaucracy was staffed by specially recruited slaves. Slave armies in the Muslim world – like the Jannisaries of the Ottoman Empire, the Mamluks in Egypt, or the elite black guards, the 'abid, in Morocco – often found themselves in the position of making and unmaking sultans, simply because they had the power to do so.

South of the Sahara, the position of slaves was similar but far more various. The northern fringe of the West African savanna was largely Muslim by the fifteenth century. It therefore constituted a mixed case between North Africa and much of the rest of the continent. But the underlying environmental conditions were different. West Africa was chronically underpopulated; land had little value without people to work it. A kinship or other group could increase its power and wealth only by adding people, and the most readily available way to add people quickly was by purchase. The owner often wanted to assimilate the slave to a kinship position, even though it was a subordinate one. In many African socieities, this subordination was only transitional, until the slave could be assimilated into the group. In some cases, slaves could become freedmen in one generation and even rise to positions of leadership. Slaves in West Africa did all kinds of work. Some were commanders of the armies or palace servants on the Muslim model. Many were concubines or wives. Others did agricultural labor, sometimes under daily instruction, but sometimes under their own direction, owing nothing but a kind of rent.

But this variety of position belonged only to settled slaves. West African societies made a sharp distinction between trade slaves and settled slaves. A freshly captured slave or a freshly condemned criminal had no rights. His life was forfeit, and the master could do as he liked. For a few months, each newly captured slave would live as a trade slave, but sooner or later the merchant/owner would sell him to Europeans or North Africans on the coast or sahel, or else sell him into West African slavery far from home. From that time, the purchaser began trying to assimilate the newcomer. If he accepted his new position, he gradually won membership in the new group and the protection of the laws. He could be resold – but other members of the group could often be sold as well, in time of famine, for example. Economic factors also discouraged resale. A trade slave, recently captured, was a potential danger to his captor. The captor often sold him or her at a low price, almost always less than the cost of supporting a child to the age of fourteen or so, when working life began. After assimilation, however, the slave was worth far more to his new society.

The beginning of the Atlantic trade

Most histories tend to treat the slave trade as it was at its height in the eighteenth of nineteenth centuries. We therefore tend to think of slaves as Africa's only export, or at least the main export until well into the nineteenth century. In fact, slaves were comparatively unimportant during the first two centuries of maritime contact – roughly the period of 1450 to 1650 A.D. The Portuguese mariners went down the coast looking for gold, not slaves. The availability of slaves for sale was a fortuitous and unexpected by-product of the gold trade. Yet the first centuries of trade were important, because they established the relationships that continued into the period of more extensive trade that was to follow.

From the first, the lure of gold concentrated Portuguese attention on two points on the West African coast. They could reach the gold fields of Buré and Bambuhu most easily from trading stations on the Gambia River. The Portuguese seized the uninhabited Cape Verde Islands offshore as a secure entrepôt for that trade. The lower Gambia was already important in West African trade as a source of sea salt, and an existing trade route carried it into the interior. Slaves were available for sale on the Gambia, and the Portuguese began to buy them, though the numbers were not large – perhaps 1,300 a year exported to Europe before 1500 A.D. and another 500 a year to the Atlantic islands (not counting São Tomé).

The second point of coastal contact was the Gold Coast as an entry to the Akan gold fields. In 1480 A.D., the Portuguese began building a trade castle at Elmina to protect the gold awaiting shipment. There too, a slave trade was already in progress, but the Akan were interested in buying slaves, not selling them.

The Portuguese obliged by entering the coastal slave trade. They already traded with the important African kingdoms at Benin and Kongo, both of which had slaves for sale. By the 1520s, São Tomé's own sugar industry had begun to grow, and the island made a convenient center for the slave trade as well. São Tomé imported about 2,000 slaves a year from all sources. The Portuguese on the island put some of them to work on local sugar plantations, and sold about 500 a year to the Akan on the Gold Coast and a few to Portugal as well. Slave shipments from Africa directly to the Americas did not begin until 1532 – to the Spanish West Indies and, still later, to Brazil.

The opening up of the Brazil market for slaves was more significant than mere distances on the map may indicate. The long east–west coast of West Africa has a strong ocean current and prevailing winds from the west. To reach either Europe or the West Indies, a sailing vessel had to drop south of the equator to catch the southeast trades, then cross the equator once more in midocean to catch the northeast trades for the main Atlantic

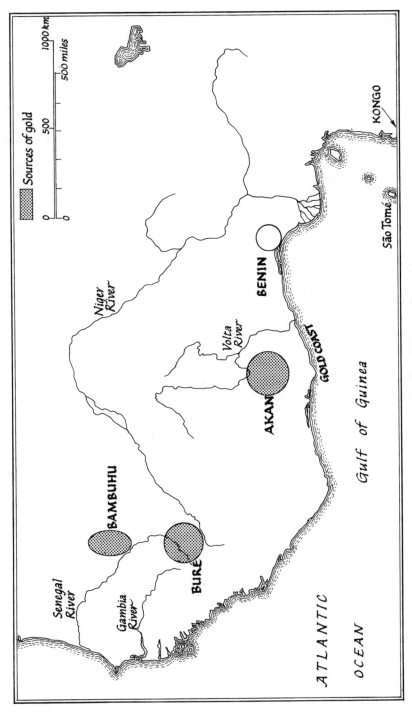

Figure 3.3   West African trading regions.

crossing – or go north to the Azores for the westerlies that would carry it to Europe. Each crossing of the equator meant passing through a belt of calms, the doldrums, which greatly increased the time required for the voyage.

After about 1550, however, the situation changed. Political disturbance in the kingdom of Kongo increased the supply of slaves; the beginning of the Brazilian sugar industry increased the demand. The voyage to the new sugar plantations was a straight run with the southeast trades, far shorter and more predictable than the trip to the West Indies. This gave Brazil an early advantage over the Caribbean. Brazilian sugar had to travel farther to reach Europe, but Brazil had easier access to African labor.

Suggestions for further reading

Ajayi, J. F., and Michael Crowder, *History of West Africa*, 2 vols., 3rd. ed. (London: Longman, 1985).

Connah, Graham, *African Civilizations. Precolonial Cities and States in Tropical Africa: An Archaeological Perspective* (Cambridge: Cambridge University Press, 1987).

Curtin, Philip D., *Cross-Cultural Trade in World History* (New York: Cambridge University Press, 1984), pp. 15–59.

Lovejoy, Paul E., *Transformations in Slavery: A History of Slavery in Africa* (Cambridge: Cambridge University Press, 1983).

Kopytoff, Igor, "African Slavery as an Institution of Marginality," in Suzanne Miers and Igor Kopytoff, *Slavery in Africa: Historical and Anthropological Perspectives* (Madison: University of Wisconsin Press, 1977), pp 3–81.

4

Capitalism, feudalism, and sugar planting in Brazil

Brazil was peculiarly important in the history of the plantation complex. In our ethnocentric way, many of us tend to think of the United States as the place where most slaves were landed. If fact, it was Brazil. Brazil was also the place where the characteristic elements of New World tropical slave plantations were first put together. Finally, in 1888 Brazil was the last country in the Western Hemisphere to abolish slavery.

Feudalism and capitalism

The early plantation complex in Brazil contained some institutional survivals from the medieval Mediterranean, as well as other institutions created for the new conditions of the New World. The Portuguese brought techniques for planting cane and making sugar from Madeira, but they also brought late feudalism and early capitalism from Europe. "Feudalism" has so many different means that precision is easily lost. In the strictest sense, "feudal" meanings "pertaining to a fief." A fief in northwestern Europe, beginning in about the eleventh century, was a gift of valuable, income-producing property – usually control over land and peasants – in return for military service. It was therefore the basis of a special and close relationship between two members of the military aristocracy. He who gave the fief established his superiority, but both were honored members of a medieval elite.

That narrow meaning was hardly relevant in sixteenth-century Portugal or Brazil, where the power of the monarchy over all of its subjects already overshadowed the military relations between them. For sixteenth-century Brazil, it makes more sense to take one of the broader meanings of feudalism, one that defines it as the exercise of political command or government power as a personal property right, rather than as a public function performed by the sovereign authority or one of his agents. This is the meaning of feudalism when a monarch granted political authority over a newly won country to those who were about to conquer it. If a king granted a noble or a member of his own family the right to collect taxes or to hold court, these rights were often hereditary, and they were feudal in this manner. The noble family *owned* the powers of government as an explicit gift from the government. This can be thought of as feudalism from above.

Feudalism from below came about when private subjects simply usurped powers that were normally those of government. In the earlier, anarchic centuries of the European Middle Ages, important militalry leaders had begun to hold courts, collect tolls, or carry out other government functions simply because they were strong enough to do so. Over time, the stolen rights became property by custom, and hence by law.

"Capitalism" is another word that needs clarification, especially in an intellectual world where institutions called "capitalist" in one century are very different from those called capitalist in another – where some historians trace capitalism back several centuries before the sixteenth, while others deny that it came fully into existence until about 1800.

One of the simplest definitions is that of capitalism as an economic system in which those who provide the capital control the production of goods. They manage the firm and make the crucial decisions about what should be produced and how. They are also entitled to the residual profits after other factors of production – land and labor – have been paid for at the rate established by supply and demand in the marketplace.

In early modern Europe, capitalism first became important to commercial operations. Those who drew dues and other payments from agiculture rarely controlled production. The landlord was not a farm manager. He simply collected dues from those who carried out farming along customary lines. In England, for example, most historians date the beginning capitalist agriculture from the time when landowners began to enclose the open, communally managed fields in order to set up sheep farms managed by themselves.

Distinctions between feudalism and capitalism may seem inconsequential, but they become more than matters of definitional hairsplitting for the followers of Karl Marx. The Marxist scheme of history has a feudal stage, followed by a capitalist stage, to be followed by a socialist stage. If you are not sure whether you are dealing with capitalism or feudalism in a particular circumstance, you cannot know what the future course of history will be. I prefer to avoid the Marxist debate by avoiding the Marxist meaning of feudalism. Marx wrote in the nineteenth century, when the feudalism in the recent past no longer involved relations between those who gave and those who received fiefs. For Marx, the essence of the feudal mode of production was the fact that members of the military class had become landholders, whose control over the land gave them the right to extract income from the semiservile peasants who worked it.

Intentions and experiments in Brazil

These distinctions are, of course, historians' hindsight. The earliest Portuguese to conduct business in Brazil had only a small idea of what they wanted and how they might get it, much less whether it was capitalist or feudal. They did not even know at first that Brazil was to become a natural extension of the plantation complex already present in the Algarve of Portugal itself or on Madeira. Brazil was, first and foremost, a place the Portuguese had to pass on the way to India. Once past the bulge of Africa and the doldrums, the most direct route to the Cape of Good Hope was in the teeth of southeast trade winds. To avoid this, mariners sailed as close to the trades as possible – just as those headed back toward Europe took a detour away from the Saharan coast of Africa. As a result, they passed very close to the northeastern bulge of Brazil. In the first decades of the sixteenth century, the Portuguese thought of their Atlantic trade in two separate segments. The African gold trade was one; the spice trade around the Cape of Good Hope to India and the spice islands was another. Brazil was part of the route to India, but only as a useful stopover.

In the beginning, Brazil had very little to offer. It had no useful products for export – no gold or spices for sale. It only offered a place where ships could get fresh fruit, fresh water, and a little dye wood growing wild in the forests. For three decades (say, 1500 to 1530), the Portuguese who sailed along the Brazilian coast made no attempt that could be called empire building of any kind. Ships stopped for wood and water. From time to time, a ship might drop off a man between trips to buy dye woods and thus reduce the turnaround time for the ship on its way home. Whatever law and government existed were supplied by the Indians – though the political structures in that part of South America were minimal. Nor were the Portuguese alone; other European nations, the French in particular, were in the Brazil trade on about the same basis. Commercial exchange was barter. The Europeans took out European goods and exchanged them for Indian labor. The Indians then cut the wood in the forest and piled it on the shore for loading.

This kind of cross-cultural exchange was a little like the Indian Ocean trading systems without the fortified trade enclaves. But it was very different from the Spanish way of dealing with the Indians of the Caribbean, Mexico, and Peru. There the Europeans came in with their military power out front. They wanted material rewards, as the Portuguese did in Brazil, but they chose force as the means to that end.

Without the known gold and silver of Mexico and Peru or the spices of Indonesia, Brazil attracted a different kind of European. The military nobility went off to become *conquistadores* in the eastern seas. Those attracted to Brazil were mere merchants. They made contracts with the Casa da India, which ran the overseas business affairs of the Portuguese crown, but these contracts were not feudal charters authorizing personal government over land that might be conquered. They merely granted the right to trade. Some private individuals signed up, but so did some syndicates with several members. Some were New Christians (recently converted Jews), and some were not even Portuguese – the crown being less nationalistic about Brazil than about more obviously valuable overseas territories. Anyone could trade, so long as the crown received its determined share.

A second phase opened in 1534 after European rivals appeared on the coast. The French had sent a few ships for dye woods and refused to pay the Portuguese crown for the priviledge. Portugal answered with a royal naval expedition in 1530 and switched to a new policy. More accurately, it switched from no policy to the kind of policy it had already used for the Atlantic islands.

The government divided the whole coast of Brazil into strips marked off by straight lines running west from approximately equal stretches of the Atlantic coast. It assigned each strip to a Portuguese individual or company under a feudal charter giving full powers to the grantee. (The crown could afford to be generous, since it was giving away what it did not yet own.) The grantees bore the title "captain donatory." Hence, the new colonies were called *capitanías donatarios*. Within his jurisdiction, the captain had the legal right to do almost anything. As a virtual sovereign, he controlled everything except the church; the only judicial power he lacked was that of carrying out death sentences against nobles. He could found towns and give them charters for municipal government; he could appoint all the officials; he could collect taxes at will; he could subinfeudate if he wanted. And the grants were given in perpetuity. Even if a captain was convicted of treason and executed, his heirs would still inherit his powers. In return, all the king received was the right to collect certain customs duties; a monopoly over trade in certain drugs, spices, and dye woods; and one-fifth of any gold, silver, or precious stones that might be found.

These grants were curious even for their time. They gave away exactly the powers that most European monarchs were trying to get back from the nobility at home. They reserved to the crown the economic advantages a merchant might normally want – not a king. They were also curious from another point of view. One would expect feudal grants to be given to the feudal nobility, but this was not the case. Some captains donatory were *fidalgos*, or members of the local gentry of Portugal, but many belonged to nonfeudal classes. They were the kind of people who were normally opposed to feudal powers at home – a factor in the Casa da India, a secretary from the royal treasury, a group of merchants. The practice was thus a continuation of the practice of giving feudal grants to nonfeudal grantees that marked the Mediterranean sugar industry as far back as its early decades on Cyprus.

Perhaps the experiment with *capitanías donatarios* is not so important, since it failed miserably within twenty years, but it is instructive in showing the persistence of Mediterranean traditions of colonial government. The failure itself came about because the crown wanted to found colonies on the cheap, and that was no longer possible in the sixteenth-century Atlantic basin. The captaincies were undercapitalized. They were continually short of labor, because the Indians were dying out all along the coast. They were not even much use against the French interlopers, because the captains donatory were too poor to defend their territory. The captains donatory failed financially and faded from the picture one by one. Their powers then reverted to the crown, and the captaincies became royal provinces with royal officials in place of the former grantees.

The failure of the captains donatory ended the Portuguese effort to improve feudal institutions from above. From then on, the colony was to be run by a royal bureaucracy – at least at the central level – and whatever feudal elements developed had their origins in the social and economic setting of the sugar plantation, not in government intention. The switch to crown government began in 1549, and it represented a third phase in Portuguese relations with Brazil. The shift was achieved by buying out the donatory who controlled Bahia and turning it into a royal province. A captain-general under direct orders from Lisbon acted as governor in Bahia. He also coordinated the defense of all of Portugal's American possessions and exercised whatever powers the crown had in the individual captaincies.

The sugar industry

In the middle decades of the sixteenth century, Brazil passed through a major economic shift. Sugar replaced dye woods and other forest products as the prinicpal export. Earlier experiments with sugar had been carried out with small mills up and down the Brazilian coast. As elsewhere, the earliest operations were based on technology from Madeira, but this time the principal labor force was Amerindian slaves. Even after the crown made enslavement of Indians illegal in 1570, the practice continuedunder a variety of legal guises.

But Indian slavery was not a possible long-term solution. Local Indian populations began to die out on contact with European and African diseases. A regular and substantial slave trade then began to drain population from the interior, but these men and women also died at rates far too high to become a self-sustaining population. Gradually, over the second half of the sixteenth century, a labor force of coerced Africans began to replace the labor force of coerced native Americans. By the end of the sixteenth century, Brazil emerged as the world leader in sugar production, replacing São Tomé, Madeira, and the Canaries as the chief source of European sugar – just as the Atlantic Islands had earlier replaced the Mediterranean colonies.

Several factors helped to account for this success. One was basic resource endowment. Brazil had large quantities of flat land with good soil close to the shore. This last was important because even semirefined sugar was expensive to move overland. Bahia was especially favored because, as its name suggests, the capital city of Salvador was on a large bay surrounded by some of the best and best-placed cane land in the world, called the recôncavo. This favored region was about 4,000 square miles, about the size of the island of Jamaica or three-quarters of the size of Connecticut.

Brazil was also second only to São Tomé in its access to slaves from Africa. Mortality at sea on the voyages from Angola to Brazil was normally 30 to 50 percent less than it was on voyages from Angola to the Caribbean. Lower mortality meant more slaves delivered, and hence a lower transportation cost per slave.

Brazil also had the continuing clean-slate advantage over older plantation areas. In Madeira, for example, the ordinary sugar mill produced about 15 metric tons of sugar a year, and the earliest Brazilian mills produced about the same amount. But with new land, larger scale was possible. By the 1570s, the sugar mills in Brazil produced about 30 to 130 tons. By 1600, the average was up to 130 tons a year. Bigger mills were more efficient, but these economies of scale were possible only with new plantations.

The Portuguese sugar industry also profited from the old connection between Madeira and Antwerp. This link introduced Antwerp to the business of sugar refining and brought Madeira into contact with one of Europe's richest sources of capital. As the sugar moved south and west, the Antwerp capital went with it, and Flemish capitalists financed the early expansion of sugar in Brazil. Capital was always a problem for new sugar works; the mill itself was very expensive, and the prospective planter had to lay out capital to purchase labor as well. Comtemporaneous estimates put the cost of the slaves at about 20 percent of the capital costs beyond the investment in land itself.

By 1600 in Brazil, the economic structure of the later plantation complex was nearly complete. The economy was now highly specialized, concentrated on a single crop, with most labor done by slaves – though many of the slaves were still Indians, not Africans. In short, Brazil, which had begun in the legal mold of the feudal charters, had turned for its political forms to a centralized government bureaucracy and was tied economically to the most advanced region of capitalist Europe.

Feudalism from below

Even as Brazil cast off official feudalism, another form of feudalism begin to emerge from below. This was the appropriation of governmental powers – not by gift but by usurpation, as members of the planter class began to take over powers that belonged to the royal government in Portugal itself. Given the conventional opposition of feudalism and capitalism, it may appear paradoxical that the Brazilian plantations became more capitalistic and more feudal at the same time.

The Brazilian sugar industry of the seventeenth century was certainly capitalist. The planters owned the land, they owned the tools – the sugar mills – and they owned the labor. They planned production in a rational way to maximize their profit. But a sugar plantation was also a society consisting of 100 to 300 people – even more in later centuries. The plantations were scattered throughout the countryside in a new country where the web of government was not yet capable of dealing with individuals. These small societies needed some form of government. It was only natural for the *senhor de engenho*, or master of the sugar factory, to begin settling quarrels, punishing offenders against the common interest, and taking on the powers that were otherwise those of police and magistrates' courts. The same was the case, though to a smaller degree, of the *laboradores de canha*, the cane farmers who worked the land with their slaves and sold the cane to the *engenhos*.

Some such thing might have taken place, even if the workers were free people working for wages; but most of the people on any sugar estate or *fazenda* were legally the property of the *fazendeiro*.Ownership carried with it the right to punish the slaves. The estates were self-contained and nearly self-sufficient in food, and the royal government was too far away to exercise effective control. Other extralegal changes took place as well. Indians were not supposed to be enslaved, but the slave trade from the interior continued well into the seventeenth century. Indians voluntarily attracted to the estates by the lure of wages often found themselves assimilated to the class of slaves, whether Amerindian or African.

Within a few decades, a new class structure emerged, often assimilating the names of class positions in Portugal but actually reflecting the way individuals were associated with the estate and the production of sugar. The individual capitalist owner might be deeply in debt to an Antwerp merchant house, but locally he was *the* owner and head of a community – though with higher status for the owners of the sugar mills than for mere cane farmers.

Though deriving a bundle of powers from his position of the *fazenda*, the planter also lost some of his power to control production. Capitalist ownership still gave him legal rights, but the passage of time made these harder and harder to enforce. Two or three generations away from the original founder, his heirs no longer had *in fact* the full freedom to act like capitalist entrepreneurs. They and the whole *engenho* were caught in a web of customary relationships between individuals playing fixed roles in this miniature society. Social pressures forced the *fazendeiro* to act in prescribed ways toward his family, his mistress, his children (both free and slave), his employees, and his slaves. Economic pressures circumscribed his freedom to change the production function. He could not easily increase the size of the estate – a "dirty slate disadvantage" equivalent to the clean slate advantage of a new settlement. He could not easily change the crop. He could not lay off workers, since the workers were owned, not hired. The workers too were bound by the traditions and customs of plantation life, creating expectations that the master had to fulfill, at least to some degree.

By about 1600, the Brazilian sugar planter had become as institution-bound and custom-bound as the European lord of the manor had been during the Middle Ages. He was no longer a capitalist innovator, free to change and move as rational calculation of his alternative possibilities indicated. He was a capitalist in the sense that he was tied to European capital markets by a web of loans. His product went there for sale. Supply and demand and the play of the market were effective forces in establishing the plantation's annual income, but the *fazendeiro* could respond only with difficulty.

Local government

Feudalism from below also penetrated the structure of local government. The tradition of Portuguese local government went back to Roman practices. Local government under the Roman Empire had been an amalgamation of city-states, or *civitates*. Each ruled the surrounding rural territory, so that every scrap of territory belonged to some city, just as every scrap of New England belongs to some town. With the fall of Rome, the *civitates* kept much of their strength in the Mediterranean basin, though they weakened in northern Europe, where the feudal nobility often dominated the countryside. Towns in medieval Portugal continued as self-governing units, directly under the king and independent of the feudal nobility. The Portuguese carried this institution to Brazil. The captains donatory had the right to found new towns, and these towns had legal control over the surrounding countryside.

But urban-centered local government changed in Brazil. Except for major colonial centers, towns were small, and the local elite lived on their *fazendas*. The key municipal institution was the council or *senado da câmara*. It was not elected by popular vote but chosen in various ways to represent the "good men" *(homens bons)* of the vicinity. In northeastern Brazil of the sixteenth century, this meant the sugar planters; merchants were normally excluded, along with the urban proletariat.

The *senados da câmara* thus made it possible for the rural elite to dominate the towns. Having already usurped some government authority over the estates themselves, they could now sit in their corporate capacity as members of the *senado* to act on behalf of the planting class as a whole. They became involved in continuous political tussels with royal officials, who found them hard to control. Many *senados* maintained their own representative in Lisbon to work for their interests at court. A crown official in Brazil thus confronted entrenched local privilege that simultaneously worked behind his back.

Once under planter control, the *senados* could extend their power over local police and militia. The *capitão mor,* or captain major, was an ancient Portuguese military office. It had once been the military title that went with the governorship, in much same way that the president of the United States is commander-in-chief of the armed forces, but it sank in importance over the years. By the eighteenth century, it was only the title of the local militia commander, but the right of appointment to that office now belonged to the *senados da câmara.* The title then carried power. Its holder was theoretically the king's agent to ensure the preservation of public order. Since the royal official had lost the power of appointment, the *capitão* could use his athority in almost any way the *senado* approved. It gave the planters command over a military force – separate from royal forces – that could be used to suppress uppity slaves or free blacks or to keep poor whites in line. In some hands, it was simply a way to make anything a big planter wanted to do legal, with little or no effective check from the courts or royal officials.

Thus, over the period from the mid-sixteenth century to the mid-eighteenth, overt and official feudalism disappeared. Simultaneously, freewheeling capitalist entrepreneurship gave way to a society of status and custom. The *fazendeiros* gained power against the royal government, but they lost real control over their economic enterprise. Feudalism from above was abolished, only to appear from below – largely as a political reflection of power relationships of a rural society, where the dominant social and economic unit was the slave plantation. With variants, these powers of feudalism from below were to reappear in the Caribbean when the plantation complex moved on to the northwest in the seventeenth century.

Suggestions for further reading

Alden, Dauril, *Royal Government in Colonial Brazil* (Berkeley: University of California Press, 1968).

Hemming, John, *Red Gold: The Conquest of the Brazilian Indians, 1500–1760* (Cambridge: Harvard University Press, 1978)

Johnson, Harold B., "The Donatary Captaincy in Perspective: Portuguese Backgrounds to the Settlement of Brazil," *Hispanic-American Historical Review,* 52:203–14 (1972).

Marchant, Alexander, *From Barter to Slavery: The Economic Relations of Portuguese and Indians in the Settlement of Brazil, 1500–1580* (Baltimore: Johns Hopkins University Press, 1942).

Russell-Wood, A. J. R., *The Black Man in Slavery and Freedom in Colonial Brazil* (London: Macmillan, 1982).

Schwartz, Stuart B., *Sugar Plantations in the Formation of Brazilian Society, 1550–1835* (Cambridge: Cambridge University Press, 1985), pp. 1–98.

5

Bureaucrats and free lances in Spanish America

The post-Columbian opening of the Americas created opportunities and raised problems for European governments. The previous isolation of the Americas left them open to European conquest. The impact of European diseases made conquest easy, though the later die-off of the Indians greatly reduced the value of the prize. One problem, recurrent throughout the sixteenth and seventeenth centuries, was to create institutions capable of governing the conquered territorial empires. Another was to keep overseas Europeans under control. The growth of feudalism from below in Brazil was one manifestation of that problem. The Spanish met another in their effort to erect Spanish kingdoms on the ruins of the Aztec and Inca empires. The British, French, and Dutch were to encounter still others in the Caribbean when they sought to establish their own versions of the plantation complex.

True colonies were no easier to control, as the British found out when the thirteen North American colonies seceded in the 1780s – and as the United States discovered in the 1860s when the slave states tried to secede in their turn. Both secessions, successful or unsuccessful, were associated with the dissolution of the plantation complex. Though distant in time, they were also related to the conflict between military conquerors and imperial bureaucrats in the first decades of Spain's conquest of the American mainland.

Frontiers: freedom and anarchy versus despotism and slavery

The terms "bureaucrat" and "free lance" are ways of expressing two opposing forces that are recurrent on the fringes of European expansion overseas. One of these is a tendency toward government control, despotism, and serfdom or slavery for large segments of the working class; Russian serfdom and the slavery of the plantation complex are type cases. The second tendency is toward an unusual degree of freedom, if not anarchy. The North American frontiersman, exemplified in American folklore by Daniel Boone and Davy Crocket, is one type case. Cowboys, *coureurs de bois* in Canada, cossacks on the Russian steppe, and gauchos on the pampas are others. European commentators in the nineteenth century made much of these contrasting tendencies in the United States. They could set the slavery in the South against what they often saw as outrageous degrees of democracy and freedom, if not outright lawlessness, among white southerners and frontiersmen elsewhere. Some, like Alexis de Tocqueville, were mildly tolerant, but others, like E. Gibbon Wakefield, the British theorist of colonization, looked at the combination of undue freedom and undue servitude and called Americans a people "who had become rotten before they were ripe."

These two tendencies – toward extra strong government and toward no government at all – are perhaps natural to any frontier situation. Medieval monarchs recognized that feudal lords near the borders of the kingdom needed to have more military strength than was desirable for the nobility in general. The lords of the marches could defend the borders, but the court found them hard to control. This situation was recurrent in Europe during the Middle Ages and is reflected in the use of special titles, like "marquis" and "margraf," for marcher lords.

The crown and the bureaucracy

Similar conditions existed on the frontier against the Muslims of the Iberian Peninsula. In a schematic way, the princes of northern Spain tried consistently to build a stronger bureaucratic state in the face of opposition from the feudal nobility. They were reasonably successful up to the mid-thirteenth century, when the drive for the reconquest was at its height, but many important heroes of the reconquest were free lances who conquered on their own, not as officers in a royal army. El Cid, of literary fame, was a model of the type. Then, when the Iberian frontier stopped moving – when the danger to the south was removed – royal power decreased and that of the nobility increased. Some rulers, indeed, conceded powers to the nobility as the price of keeping their own claim to office. Social and military tension between the towns and the nobility also increased.

Weakening of central government made the Spanish kingdoms less effective in the face of chronic warfare in France from the middle of the fourteenth century to the middle of the fifteenth – the period of the Hundred Years' War. Toward the middle of the fifteenth century, the French monarchy recovered enough power to control its own military class, but many of the fighting men who could no longer operate freely in France moved to Spain and contributed to the disorder that already existed there. These fifteenth-century conditions in Iberia were an important background for the conquest of America. In effect, the two groups that were to oppose one another in sixteenth-century Mexico and Peru were already opposed to one another in Spain itself. On the one hand were the military who had fought the wars – not so much the old nobility as the free companies, made up of free lances in the original sense of the term, fighting men who would fight for whoever paid best or for whatever gain they found in it for themselves. On the other hand was the power of the crowns of Aragon, Castile, and Portugal, the only available rallying points against disorder, and royal power meant more than the mere power of the kings as the greatest feudal lords. It also meant the power of a new group of legally trained bureaucrats.

In the reign of Ferdinand and Isabella, strong government reemerged. Ferdinand had a claim to be king of Aragon. Isabella had a claim to Castile. They married and united the claims, inheriting Castile in 1474 and Aragon in 1479. It took several decades of warfare to make these claims good, but in 1492 they completed the territorial unity of what was to become the Spanish monarchy by conquering Granada, the one remaining Muslim principality.

Meanwhile Ferdinand and Isabella set out to build a strong and centralized monarchy – creating the institutions their successors were to export to the Americas and using a variety of resources. One of these was the church. Because of Spain's position on the frontiers of Christendom, the Spanish princes had had much greater authority over the church than was common elsewhere in Europe. They were considered to have what was called "particular patronage" over certain church offices, which meant in effect that appointments to those offices were made by the Spanish crown rather than the church hierarchy. They first used their authority within the church to reform the church itself, acting through Cardinal Francisco Ximenes de Cisneros, the primate of Spain. The first objective was the reform of the religious orders – institutional, not doctrinal, reform – though the impetus was to continue into the sixteenth century, when it merged with the broader Catholic Reformation. This was, incidentally, the first church reform in Europe – antedating the Protestant Reformation. The important fact, however, is that this reform was forced on the church by the monarchy, partly for secular reasons.

One aspect of the Italian Renaissance had been the revival of Roman law, and Roman law was more favorable to the powers of the state than any of the medieval customary laws in Europe had been. Churchmen at first and then laymen as well trained in Roman law (*letrados* in Castile) made excellent servants of the crown, and they became the bureaucrats par excellence at this period – just as the ex-Jewish scholarly class had been the principal bureaucrats earlier in Spanish history.

The use of state power to reform the church led to the use of the church as an institution behind which all Spaniards could unite. Crown bureaucrats sought religious unity by playing on popular anti-Semitism. They and the crown sought to convert all Jews to Christianity. They also used the Spanish Inquisition – a state agency, not a church agency like the Roman Inquisition. The crown created it; a royal council controlled it. It was designed to help reform the church, to strengthen the state, to purify the laity, and to convert or to expel the Jews and *mudejares*, or Muslim Spaniards.

All of this activity was carried on in spite of opposition from unruly elements like the fuedal nobility and the free companies, and their traditions were slow to die. The crown did, however, act in ways that made anarchy more difficult. The military religious orders, which had been one source of disorder, were brought under royal control. The towns joined in against the forces of anarchy, founding the Santa Hermandad, a new kind of military order, a militia or police force to oppose the nobility and to root out banditry and lawlessness in the countryside – not to fight the Moors.

By the 1490s, when the fighting for Spanish unification was complete, fighting men of the free-lance category found small employment in Spain itself. People who wanted to live by the sword had to go elsewhere. Spain in effect exported the free lances, just as France had done a half-century earlier. Some went to the Italian wars, which were virtually constant from 1495 to 1559. Others went to the Americas, where a man could both win something for himself and escape from the tightening grip of monarchic restraint.

Intentions and achievements in the American world

Castile, like Portugal, had an Atlantic coast, but the Spanish court looked toward the Mediterranean, with special concern about southern Italy. That fitted Aragon's long-term interests. With Columbus' voyages, the court recognized that new possibilities had opened on the Atlantic, but it was not very clear just what those possibilities might be. The crown therefore began with a full feudal grant to the Columbus family – roughly equivalent to the grants later given by Portugal to the captains donatory – virtual control over all they could conquer.

Full as this grant was, it promised no royal assistance; it implied no early Spanish intention to found a true empire in the New World. The recent past contained no precedent for territorial empire in any case. Both Spain and Portugal had acquired trading cities along the Moroccan and Algerian coasts whenever the opportunity occurred. Portugal founded similar fortified trading posts in sub-Saharan Africa, and it did the same in India after 1500. Some historians have hinted that the conquest of the New World was largely a continuation of the *reconquista* of southern Iberia, but the crown made no plans for a true empire overseas. The evidence in favor of a trading post empire is much stronger. (If royal money was to be invested in territorial acquisition, Italy was the goal of proven value.) In 1503, the crown set up the Casa de Contratación, or house of trade, a direct copy of the Casa da India in Lisbon. It was originally intended to carry out trade on the crown's account and for royal profit. American trading posts, however, showed little immediate value, and the Casa became a regulatory agency. Spain dropped out of the trading post business until a small opening occurred some decades later in the Philippines. Instead of attracting merchants, the American tropics – and initially this meant only the Caribbean – attracted the kinds of people who could profit from conditions there. It attracted the free lances, who organized themselves as war bands to capture whatever booty they could find.

The West Indies

Unlike most of the Americas, the Caribbean was relatively densely populated. The three large islands of Jamaica, Hispaniola, and Puerto Rico were inhabited by the Arawak, an agricultural people, living in organized states with a marked class structure, occupational specialization and division of labor, and institutionalized religous practices. Cuba was also partly Arawak but was sparsely populated. The Arawak were not as advanced as the great civilizations of Mexico and Peru, but they were technically more skilled than most American peoples outside the highlands of the Andean chain and Middle America.

The people of the Lesser Antilles were Caribs, who were good at fighting. The Spanish left them alone and moved on to the Greater Antilles, where they found placer gold – especially on Hispaniola – and Indians less able to defend themselves. The Spanish set up their first government on Hispaniola, where they quickly abandoned the broad feudal pattern of the Columbus grant and moved toward real royal government, but the free lances were already farther out.

Small Spanish war bands had already begun to operate in the Caribbean, using Hispaniola as a base. Digging ore and panning gold from the stream beds took more labor than Hispaniola could provide – as was often the case when new mines or plantations were introduced. Laborers could be found on other islands and imported as slaves. As the local population began to die in the early epidemics of European and African disease, the labor shortage became more serious. As nearby Amerindian groups converted to Christianity, they could no longer be enslaved legally. The Spanish war bands began to raid more widely, looking for slaves on the farther islands and on the mainland. The slaves died in turn, and the war bands had to go farther still. By the end of the sixteenth century, virtually all of the Indians of the tropical lowlands were dead except the Caribs, whose fighting propensities reduced the intensity of contact and gave them a chance to develop immunities to the new diseases.

In the first phase, then, no sooner had the Spanish bureaucrats begun to establish order on Hispaniola, Jamaica, and Puerto Rico than the war bands fanned out all over the Caribbean, carrying the free-lance frontier beyond bureaucratic reach. The real battle was to be fought in the great civilizations of the highlands. There, at least, malaria and yellow fever could not go, and enough Indians could stay alive to maintain their existence as a community, even though they lost enormous numbers.

Mexico

In Mexico, the Spanish war bands arrived to raid for slaves, but they discovered something new – a large and populous urban society. The central highlands of Mexico had been settled for centuries by people who were skilled farmers with a lively art, a network of cities, a form of writing, and a complex intellectual life that has only recently been subject to serious study.

The political forms in central Mexico were those of the city-state, and one of the principal functions of the state was the organization of large forces of labor for the construction of irrigation works. But this was not a "water-works state" in the sense of Karl Witfogel's theory of some decades ago, which suggested that the political forms of "oriental depotism" had come about because societies like those of Egypt or China had serious problems of water control – either to provide water for the Egyptian desert or to prevent flooding in the Yellow River Valley of North China.[1] In theory, the size of the river system determined the scale of the state and the extent of state control over the peopple whose labor had to be mobilized. Many authorities now doubt the full force of Witfogel's

[1] Karl Witfogel, *Oriental Despotism: A Comparative Study of Total Power* (New Haven: Yale University Press, 1957).

theory, even in Asia. Mexican conditions were different. In many scattered parts of highland Mexico, irrigation could increase yields enormously, but rainfall farming was also possible. It was not necessary to have a large state to control the whole region – not, at least, for the technical needs of water control. Instead of bringing water to the land, some of the ancient Mexican irrigation techniques brought farming to the water, planting crops on platforms of wood and soil floating on shallow lakes. *Chinampas* agriculture of this kind can still be seen in Xochimilco outside Mexico City.

But central Mexico was like China in another way. It had an ecological frontier that separated it from the arid lands to the north, where intensive agriculture was impossible outside a few favored pockets of well-watered land. This was the country of the *chichimec*, as the people of central Mexico called them – "the wild people" living a seminomadic life, though with some agriculture.

One of the processes in Mexican history before the sixteenth century was a tendency for war bands to cross the *chichimec* frontier into the civilized territory to the south. Some settled down, others conquered one or more of the city-states, and still others retired after a series of destructive raids. The last invasion before the arrival of the Spanish had been that of a smallish group called the Tenochcas, who came to the valley of Mexico about 1250 A.D. They gradually came to dominate the valley of Mexico and the whole area around it. In time, they were able to transform their own system of control from the domination of a war band over city-states to a bureaucratic government that was able to unify the separate irrigation systems of the valley. This produced higher yields, economic progress, and the growth of their capital at Tenochtitlán into a city larger than any city in Spain at this time. Their government came to be called the Aztec Empire, and their capital is the site of present-day Mexico City.

But that government was administratively weak outside the valley. It sent out military expeditions and demanded tribute over a wide area, but it made little effort to exert continuous control. In this sense, the so-called empire was no empire at all. It was a military predominance of one city-state, large by Mexican standards, over its neighbors.

The arrival of the Spanish in Mexico is a familiar story.

Hernando Cortés, a law-trained free lance, organized an expedition in Cuba. It was a free company, not a Spanish army, recruited and commanded by servants of the Spanish crown, though it claimed to be acting in the interests of the crown. When the expedition arrived in the vicinity of present-day Vera Cruz, Cortés went through the legal process of incorporating the expedition as a Spanish town – thus giving it a fictional legal status so that its acts could be construed as those of a government, not a free company. But from that point on, the Spanish war band inserted itself into the existing Mexican political pattern, displacing the Tenochcas from their control of central Mexico, just as the Tenochcas' ancestors had displaced others before them. It was nevertheless an impressive victory of a few hundred men over an empire that ruled millions. Cortés's victory no doubt combined some skill and some luck, but its essence was strategic surprise – the appearance of strangers no one had known of before, with horses and guns. Cortés also worked within the Mexican system of alliances, so that the final assault on Tenochtitlán was made by an army that was mainly Mexican – not Spanish. By that time, the first epidemics had already appeared, adding disease to the ranks of the victors.

In the Spanish context, the army in Mexico claimed to be a Spanish city, with the rights a city would enjoy in Spanish law, but in reality was still a free company of the kind the Spanish crown had been trying to bring under control. In the first instance, it was not Spain that conquered Mexico, only individual Spaniards who had seized control of the Aztec domination. The next decision was whether Cortés and his war band would rule independently, behind the façade of a Spanish municipality, or whether the Spanish state could establish genuine control over these adventurers thousands of miles away. In retrospect, we see the establishment of the kingdom of New Spain, followed later by other viceroyalties, and knitted together through the Council of the Indies into an elaborate bureaucratic empire. It is important, however, not to miss the alternatives and the play of forces that led to this outcome.

In Mexico, the situation passed quickly through a series of stages. After the fall of Tenochtitlán in 1521, Cortés put himself at the head of the refounded Mexican state. In so doing, he reestablished, or continued, the political structure he had just conquered, working through the bureaucratic forms of the Indian city-states – an unusual decision for the leader of a war band. Cortés could command the support of a free company, but he had the training and attitudes of a *letrado,*who might have been just as much at home in the Spanish bureaucracy. Cortés, furthermore, acted immediately to place his new state directly under the control of the Spanish crown. Round one in Mexico, therefore, went to the bureaucrats.

But this first victory was brief: It lasted only from 1522 to 1524. During these years some of the Cortés's own men became restive. They wanted the spoils of conquest Cortés had refused to them – though Cortés himself was richly rewarded by the crown. As more free lances began arriving from Spain – some as individuals, some as partly formed free companies – the demand increased for further conquests and new spoils.

Cortés was able to control these forces until 1524, when he was called away to try to regain control over a new expedition that was penetrating Honduras. By leaving for the south, he lost control of the war bands in central Mexico. Some of the free lances, old and new, formed into groups of soldiers who began cutting out semi-feudal domains for themselves, simply seizing bits of territory and beginning to run them as private preserves. Others went off to the north, west, and south in search of new worlds to conquer.

Diseases from Europeans and Africans continued to sweep across central Mexico in a series of "virgin field" epidemics among people without acquired immunities. The epidemics made conquest easy, but they made economic recovery very difficult. This was the period when Beltrán Nuño de Guzmán conquered territory in western Mexico, which he called New Galicia, and Pedro de Alvarado went south and east along the height of land through Tehuantepec and Chiapas to conquer highland Guatemala.

Cortés returned to Mexico in 1526, but he was never able to reestablish his old power, and the Spanish governors sent out to replace him either themselves fell into the patterns and traditions of the war band or else failed to control those who did. Thus, round two went to the free lances – roughly during the period 1524–35.

Encomienda

This period of a dozen years or so was crucial for the institutions that were to prevail in the new territory, especially the *encomienda.*The war band tradition in the Antilles had been one of open enslavement of the Indians. Cortés, however, tried to prevent this, as well as the foundation of virtually independent fiefs by Spanish war captains. The *encomienda* had already been used in the Antilles as a way to forestall open slavery and private fiefdoms. An *encomienda* was, in law and theory, a grant of general jurisdiction over a group of Indian subjects, given by the crown to a private individual. That individual, the *encomendero,* was entitled to collect whatever services or taxes these Indians might owe the king. He, in turn, promised the crown to see that the Indians were properly instructed in religion, and to perform military service if called on. In law, this was not a feudal grant. It did not transfer any of the king's rights of jurisdiction over the Indians. The *encomendero* was not to rule over them, only to collect money or labor services. Nor was the *encomienda* a land grant; it therefore lacked an important economic aspect of true feudal grants. In a period of declining population, however, it was not hard to acquire land by other means, and the *encomendero* could easily make the Indians work on his holdings.

In spite of its nonfeudal character, it was apparant that the *encomienda* could be made into a genuine property right to political power by simple usurpation, not unlike the usurpation that took place on the Brazilian sugar estates. The crown's bureaucrats and lawyers opposed the institution from the beginning, just as the free-lance *conquistadores* favored it. Some officials, however, including Cortés himself, saw no way to bring the war bands under control without giving in to some of their demands. The *encomienda* in effect legalized some measure of control over the Indian population, which the free lances were about to take by force anyway. Whatever the arguments and interests on the opposite sides, *encomiendas* were granted, most fully in periods of low crown control, and crown officials were to spend the rest of the century trying to get them back into government hands.

The return of the bureaucrats

Round three began in the mid-1530s, when government servants began trying to limit the powers of the *encomenderos* and to tighten bureaucratic controls all along the line. In Mexico, it began with António de Mendoza as viceroy of New Spain. He was reasonably successful in regaining control of the central government in Mexico City and suppressing the last of the independent free lances. The long-term effort was more difficult.

This drive for bureaucratic supremacy was a long process, hardly begun in the viceroyalty of Peru until the 1570s. There and elsewhere, it involved a complex military struggle and the threatened use of force on the bureaucratic side. It elicited appeals to Spanish opinion at home by missionaries like Bartolomé de Las Casas, who called Spanish attention to the patterns of death and demographic decline among the Indians in the Antilles and the tropical lowlands. The discussions in Spain raised important questions about Spain's right to empire and the proper ends of colonial government – questions never raised before, because no one had intended to found an overseas empire in the first place.

By the end of the century, the crown won round three, but only by a close decision. By that time, however, the Indians were dying out. The native American society that the Spanish had taken over early in the century began to come apart, not so much from Spanish cruelty as from the unintended impact of disease. Estimates of the pre-Columbian American population differ greatly, which means that estimates of the population decline must differ accordingly. By the middle of the seventeenth century, as much as 90 percent of the population of central Mexico may have died without leaving descendants. Even if the population loss was only 50 to 75 percent, as some other authorities believe, it was disastrous. In the Lesser Antilles, only a few Caribs were able to preserve their life as a community. In the Greater Antilles, the Arawak disappeared as a separate culture group. They were not wiped out completely, but their descendants joined the growing numbers of Afro-Caribbean creoles, and their line was reduced to a small part in a mixed genepool of Caribbean people.

The establishment of Spanish power over its territorial empire in the Middle American and South American highlands was only the opening phase of a much longer struggle between European metropolises and their frontiers. Much of that struggle lay outside the core area of the plantation complex, and distant echoes could be heard in U.S. history in western regional resentment of East Coast economic dominance.

The important decision reached in the sixteenth century, however, was that Europeans were going to succeed in creating bureaucratic territorial empires over significant parts of the non-Western world. We take that for granted now. It was within the realm of possibility, however, that individual Spanish free lances would have created their own secondary empires in the tropical Americas – just as Leopold of Belgium and the Boer republics succeeded briefly in doing in tropical Africa during the nineteenth century. In the longer run, the successors of the free lances might not have been able to prevail against Spain alone; but alliance with England, the Netherlands, Portugal, or some other European power might well have tipped the balance. As it was at the end of the sixteenth century, Spanish power was confirmed over the tropical American highlands. Portugal had extended the plantation complex into northeastern Brazil. The future of the plantation complex – if it was to have a future beyond northeastern Brazil – depended on the way in which the northern powers moved to insert themselves into the Hispanic monopoly overseas.

Suggestions for further reading

Diaz del Castillo, Bernal, *The True History of the Conquest of Mexico* (Available in several editions.)

Knight, Franklin W., *The Caribbean: The Genesis of a Fragmented Nationalism* (London: Oxford University Press, 1978).

Newson, Linda, *Aboriginal and Spanish Colonial Trinidad: A Study in Culture Contact* (London: Academic Press, 1976).

Padden, R.C., *The Hummingbird and the Hawk: Conquest and Sovereignty in the Valley of Mexico 1503–1541* (New York: Harper & Row, 1970).

Parry, John H., *The Audiencia of New Galicia in the Sixteenth Century: A Study of Spanish Colonial Government* (Cambridge: Cambridge University Press, 1948).

Schwartz, Stuart, and James Lockhart, *Early Spanish America* (New York: Cambridge University Press, 1983).

Seventeenth-century transition

1492 Columbus

Pilgrams arrive 1620

6

The sugar revolution and the settlement of the Caribbean

For historians of the Caribbean, the "sugar revolution" usually means the seventeenth-century introduction of the whole plantation complex into the eastern Caribbean, including its technology, institutions, and the African slaves to do most of the work. "Revolution" is the right word, but that particular sugar revolution of the seventeenth century was only one among many. Each time the complex moved to a new place, it had brought on a new sugar revolution. The onward movement from Madeira to Brazil was a sugar revolution; the forward movement from the eastern Caribbean to Saint Domingue and Jamaica after 1700 was another; and still others lay in the future for Cuba, Mauritius, Natal, Peru, Hawaii, and Fiji – among others. The sugar revolution in the eastern Caribbean, however, was especially significant. It continued the institutional and economic patterns already developed in Brazil, but this new version of the plantation complex was more specialized, more dependent on networks of maritime, intercontinental communication. It was also an important step into the North Atlantic, and it was, incidentally, the stepping stone that was to bring the African slave trade and a peripheral version of the plantation complex to the United States.

Caribbean geography

The Caribbean islands are far more diverse than might be expected. A number of variables joined to make any one of them especially valuable at seventeenth-century levels of technology.

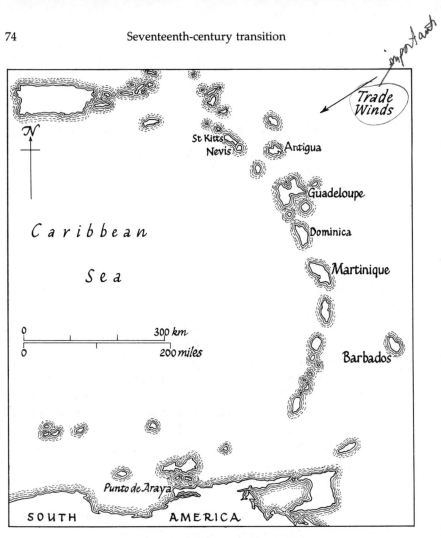

Figure 6.1   The eastern Caribbean.

Soil is obviously important, and several of these islands have fine volcanic soils, but the most valuable volcanic soils are concentrated in only a few square miles – not in regions as large as the whole of one of the Greater Antilles. Volcanoes also produce different landforms, so that Dominica – midway between Guadeloupe and Martinique, two of the richest sugar islands in the eighteenth century and equally volcanic – never became a major participant in the plantation complex for lack of enough reasonably level land.

In the seventeenth and eighteenth centuries, many of the smaller Caribbean islands had the same advantage as the Brazilian *reconcavo*. Most of the best sugar land was near the coast, so that barrels of sugar could be rolled to the beach and transshipped by lighter to seagoing vessels. Even twenty or thirty miles of land transportation could cut heavily into the potential profits. This meant that a small island's seventeenth-century advantage would be lost by the nineteenth, when railroads opened up new regions like the Cuban interior.

The distance from Europe is clear enough from looking at a globe or at most non-Mercator maps of the North Atlantic, but the sailing time to and from Europe was something else. The trade winds blew from the northeast all year round. To be upwind was a real advantage for the voyage back to Europe. Barbados was the most easterly of the Caribbean islands. A ship from Barbados bound for Europe could sail straight north on the northeast trade winds to catch the prevailing westerlies somewhere north of Bermuda. The Windward Passage between Cuba and Hispaniola is called "windward" in English because it is upwind from Jamaica. But the passage was downwind from Saint Domingue. A ship from Port-au-Prince could sail north through the Windward Passage and on to Europe, while a sailing vessel leaving Port Royal in Jamaica for Europe had the choice of either tacking laboriously upwind to the Windward Passage or sailing downwind to round the western end of Cuba in order to use the favorable current of the gulf stream to get back into the Atlantic and north along the Carolina coast. The route around Cuba was longer and involved greater danger in wartime, but it usually made for a faster passage home. As a result of these conditions, the cost of Jamaican sugar landed in Liverpool was higher than that of Barbadian sugar by about £2 to £5 sterling a ton simply because of the longer voyage, and even Saint Domingue had a marked advantage over Jamaica.

Still another important variable was rainfall, and the Caribbean islands are curious in this respect. The northeast trades carry a lot of moisture, and, blowing from comparatively cool to comparatively warm seas, they pick up still more. If these trade winds pass over a high island, their temperature drops and the water vapor is wrung out in the form of rain. The same wind can blow over a low island and drop so little rainfall as to make the island useless

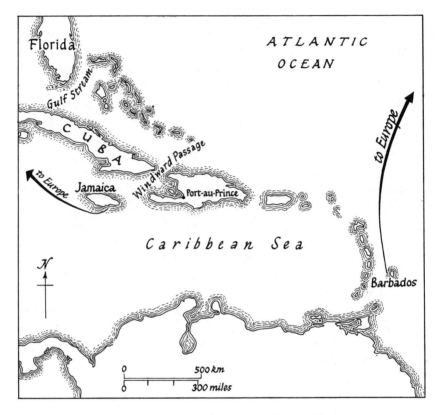

Figure 6.2   Sailing routes from the Caribbean to Europe.

for a crop like sugarcane. As a result, rainfall is highly localized. It is so low on some parts of Jamaica that agriculture is impossible without irrigation, yet at other points on the mountain crests, within sight of the semidesert, rainfall reaches an annual average of more than 200 inches a year.

In these circumstances, the ideal island for the early installation of the plantation complex was in the eastern Caribbean, high enough to bring down rainfall, relatively small for maximum access to the sea, and with some relatively flat land near the edges. St. Kitts and Nevis, Guadeloupe, and Martinique all fit this description. Antigua was also good for cane, though rainfall was sometimes irregular, and Barbados was excellent, though neither Barbados nor Antigua matched the volcanic peaks on the others.

Larger islands like Hispaniola and Jamaica would also be excellent at a second stage of development, and Cuba was to be the best of all once the transportation problem was solved.

European settlement

Given the fact that the French and English picked precisely these islands for their first settlements in the Caribbean, one might assume that they had set out to establish plantations with conscious intent, as the Dutch were soon to do by seizing northeastern Brazil. In fact, they intended something quite different – colonies for European settlement, based on a very different precedent. For the English, it was the medieval English settlements in Ireland, beginning with the "English pale" around Dublin. There the objective was to send out English settlers as a garrison for protection against the wild Irish. After a lapse of time, the English returned to this goal in the late decades of the sixteenth century. Many of the promoters most involved in American colonization – in Virginia for example – were also involved in the attempt to colonize southern Ireland. Sir Walter Raleigh, for one, recruited settlers to populate a large grant he acquired in the vicinity of Waterford.

Several in Raleigh's group associated colonization with English strategic interests in the tropical Americas. The lure was the mineral wealth of the Spanish territorial empire, but that was too strong for direct assault. The best strategy against Spain in the Americas was to form colonies – true colonies, settled by farming families who would be self-supporting and provide a loyal population for defense or offense in case of war. In addition, these true colonies would add strength to fortified trading posts in the New World, following the model of the militarized trade diasporas of the Indian Ocean. These posts would be a cross between existing colonies in Ireland or Virginia and the trading post operations of the East India Company. Though open trade with Spanish America was not possible, smuggling into Spanish territory and trade with the Amerindians would be a beginning. If all went well, some of the Indians might be persuaded to rise against Spanish oppression.

These objectives seem to have been uppermost in the mid-

1620s, when the settlement of Barbados was planned. It was to be a true colony, with plantations worked by European immigrant labor – partly to grow tobacco as a cash crop, partly as an English base for further smuggling into the Spanish Empire. From its settlement in 1627 to 1635, Barbados grew slowly, but in the second half of the 1630s it gained more immigrants than the mainland colonies. By 1640, the population was roughly the same as that of Massachusetts or Virginia, in spite of its tiny area. Both Barbados and Virginia, however, were different from Massachusetts in the sex distribution of the immigrants. Whereas Massachusetts attracted many families, the other two areas attracted few families and few women. At this stage in their history, neither had even the beginnings of a self-sustaining population. After about fifteen years, Barbados had barely reached a population of about 9,000 settlers from Europe.

French objectives in the Caribbean were similar to those of the English. Their first activities in the Americas had been trade – smuggling into the Spanish Empire and barter with the Caribs of the Lesser Antilles. Their first settlement was on Saint Christophe (later St. Kitts), which they shared for a time with the English, but their first real colonization came after 1635, with the foundation of the American Island Company.

The company was one of many founded by colonial powers in the seventeenth century. Like the others, it mixed elements of commerce with the exercise of governmental powers. Though these seventeenth-century charters were not necessarily expressed in the language of feudalism, they were essentially a reflection of feudalism from above. The French crown granted the Compagnie des isles d'Amérique jurisdiction over anything it might occupy between Trinidad to the south and central Florida to the north – though the company's actual intentions had to do with St. Kitts, Guadeloupe, and Martinique. The stockholders held formal jurisdiction, but the crown reserved the right to appoint the governor. This meant that whatever political powers the company might hold would have to be exercised under crown supervision. The stockholders, in turn, received a monopoly over trade and the right to take over the land and make it productive. To this end, they promised to introduce a minimum of 4,000 French Catholics into their colonies over the first twenty years.This first company failed financially, but its powers passed to successors – who still sought to create a settlement colony, as the English had done.

The economics of sugar and disease

The change from settlement to plantation took place for a number of reasons; some were mere accidents of time and place, whereas others were more fundamental. One of these was the economic nature of sugar as a commodity. At any date up to the late nineteenth century, all things being equal, sugar had a high price elasticity of demand. This means that, as the price decreased, people were willing and able to buy more of it. Historically, this high price elasticity lasted until people could afford to buy all they wanted, but the seventeenth-century European market for sugar was far short of that condition. In the seventeenth and eighteenth centuries, every step toward greater efficiency of production, every step toward cheaper, more secure ocean shipping, and every step toward cheaper labor costs lowered the price and increased the demand.

The new European maritime capability, pioneered by Dutch shippers since the last decades of the sixteenth century, was a factor of that kind. Cargoes with high ratios of bulk to value could now be carried economically, whereas a half-century earlier they could not. These improvements applied to the cost of bringing slaves from Africa to the New World as well. Cheaper freight rates also made possible a greater division of labor in sugar production. In the sixteenth century, Brazil had been virtually self-sufficient in food. Each plantation region produced its own food, as well as sugar for export. From the middle of the seventeenth century, islands especially well suited for sugar production could concentrate on this single crop, importing most of their food for slaves and managers from overseas.

A second fundamental condition emerged only gradually in European consciousness. This was the epidemiological difference between Europeans and Africans in the West Indies. Both the French and English colonial planners in the early seventeenth century intended the Caribbean islands to be settled by Europeans, and both took it for granted that the vast majority of the settlers would be servants. "Servants" for this purpose would be indented or *engagés*, using the legal form of engagement or indenture for a predetermined number of years (most often three or seven). The engagement contract, furthermore, could be sold to a third party without the servants' consent, and its terms could be enforced by penal sanctions. In theory, men and women bound themselves to work for a specific number of years in return for a free passage to America and a minimal standard of material support once they arrived there. In practice, young and poverty-stricken Europeans were lured into a temporary condition of semislavery.

The possibility of using African slaves was rarely considered at first. The ultimate goal was to tap the fabulous wealth of the Spanish territorial empire, and island colonies like Barbados or Martinique were to provide potential garrisons at crucial points – for trade in the short turn, for conquest in the future. For these purposes, a rural population of African slaves would have been worse than useless, a source of weakness, not strength.

But rumors based on the Portuguese experience in Brazil had already carried the word that Africans could work in the tropics, whereas Europeans could not. That belief was mistaken, but it was to have a long life and is barely dead today. It drew part of its strength from the correct observation that, though newly arrived Europeans and Africans both died in greater numbers than old residents did, the European death rate was much higher than the African. The apparent difference was race, but the effective difference was not so much heredity as immunities acquired in childhood. The West African disease environment included the normal range of Old World diseases of the kind that had killed off the Amerindians, but it also included a range of tropical diseases not present in Europe. The chief of these were yellow fever and falciparum malaria.

Acquired immunity to falciparum malaria was less effective than it was to yellow fever. Part of the reason is that falciparum malaria is actually the work of five or more different species of protozoa, each of which – and even different varieties within a single species – leaves its individual trail of immunity in the victim fortunate enough to survive. Even this is not a true immunity. The apparently immune individual shows no dramatic clinical symptoms, but he or she remains infested with the parasite. The immunity will usually last as long as the individual is periodically reinfected. Thus, even apparently immune Africans who moved from one part of Africa to another were likely to come down with malaria. Those who moved to the Americas also lost some of their immunity, but they were far more likely to survive an attack than newly arrived Europeans were.

The other common form of malaria in the Caribbean was *Plasmodium vivax*. Even for Europeans, it was rarely fatal by itself, though it was seriously debilitating and could contribute to death from other causes. Vivax malaria was altogether absent from West Africa. West Africans, moreover, have inherited protection against vivax malaria, associated with certain hemoglobin characteristics, and their ancestors carried this protection with them to the Americas.[1]

The disease and mortality data for the eastern Caribbean in the seventeenth century are uncertain, but comparable mortality data for the end of the eighteenth century and the beginning of the nineteenth show Europeans newly arrived as young adults dying at about four times the rate of newly arrived Africans in the same age group. The sparser seventeenth-century data suggest a similar difference for that period. From the point of view of a planter, given a choice of European or African servants, the choice was clear. The European servant cost about half as much as the African, but the contract ran for only three to seven years; and the individual was likely to die before it had expired. For the African, servitude was lifelong, and life was likely to be longer.

The sugar revolution   START

With these matters in the background, why did a sugar revolution occur in the eastern Caribbean in the 1640s, rather than earlier or much later? Part of the answer was the fact that the Dutch, having established a foothold in Brazil, were also willing to carry the technology of the sugar complex from there to the Caribbean. A little before 1640, some Dutch shippers appeared in the French and British Caribbean islands – first in Barbados. They offered to show

---

[1] Kenneth F. Kiple, *The Caribbean Slave: A Biological History* (Cambridge: Cambridge University Press, 1984), pp. 14–17.

the colonists how to plant sugarcane. They also offered to sell the equipment for sugar factories, to sell slaves from Africa to increase the available work force, and to buy the crop. In some cases, Dutch immigrants offered to set up sugar estates and run them.

This may seem curious behavior, since the Dutch held all of northeastern Brazil until 1645 and Pernambuco until 1654. But the Dutch who wanted to help establish a sugar industry in the eastern Caribbean were not the same Dutch who ran the Dutch West India Company or its holdings in Brazil. They were shippers, not would-be planters, and they wanted the profits they derived from trade, even if it meant infringing the legal monopoly of the Dutch company in the African trade.

A number of external events in the 1640s made an onward movement of the sugar complex profitable to various interested groups. For English planters in the Caribbean, the Civil War at home sometimes reduced the flow of servants and sometimes increased it, but it became erratic. Would-be planters were about to make a large investment in machinery and land, and that investment could only be justified if an assured and cheap supply of labor were also available. Dutch shippers were willing and able to oblige. Only the Portuguese had been active in West African trade up to that point, but the entry of the West India Company into the African trade introduced Dutch maritime circles to African commercial regions and methods. Then, in 1640, Portugal again separated from Spain. Without Spain's other responsibilities, the Portuguese were free to begin a reconquest of northeastern Brazil. This again suggested to the Dutch that they might well look elsewhere for a foothold in the plantation complex.

Meanwhile, some "Dutch" had already migrated from Brazil to the French and British Antilles. Many of these were not even of Dutch origin; they were Portuguese New Christians. In Brazil, they had resumed their old religion under the Dutch flag. They therefore had reason not to stay around to see what the Portuguese might do if they reconquered Pernambuco. Many important Sephardic Jewish families of the Caribbean today trace their presence to this migration.

The sugar revolution on Barbados occupied the two decades 1640 to 1660. In 1637, Barbados produced no sugar at all. By the

1670s, Barbados alone produced about 65 percent of the sugar consumed in England. By 1645, 40 percent of the island was planted in sugar. By 1767, the proportion had risen to 80 percent, which meant that virtually all land useful for agriculture of any kind was devoted to this one crop.

The clean slate of a new territory made it possible for planters to organize their affairs a little differently from the Brazilian pattern. There, the sugar mill (engenho) was a separate operation that might or might not serve the lands of a single owner. Smaller farmers (lavradores de cana) grew the cane, with the assistance of their slaves, and sold it to the mill. In Barbados, the typical estate was a land unit that supplied a single mill, usually about 200 acres. If an owner had more land, he might set up several mills served by several slave gangs. By 1680, a new social structure had come into existence. In place of many smallholders working a few acres of tobacco each, the island was dominated socially, economically, and politically by the great planters. These men, 175 of whom held more than 60 slaves each, owned collectively more than half of the land and half of the slaves. As planting moved forward in the Caribbean, ownership of land and slaves was to become even more concentrated.

An estimated 30,000 people who had neither land nor capital for large-scale planting left Barbados for other colonies between 1645 and the end of the century, but thousands more came to take their place, and the overseas European population stabilized at about 20,000 from the 1650s to the 1770s. The really indicative figure is that for African slaves, who were roughly equal in number to the whites in 1655. By the 1680s, they totalled 50,000. By the 1680s, Barbados had begun to look demographically like a mature plantation colony, with about the same balance of slaves to free persons, or blacks to whites, that it was to have throughout the eighteenth century – 25 percent white and 75 percent black, with one slave for every two arable acres of land.

Given the island's small size and comparatively small population today, it is hard to keep its past importance in perspective. As of the 1680s, however, its population was larger than that of either Massachusetts or Virginia. With a population density of 400 per square mile, it was four times as densely settled as England. Given the fact that almost all of its principal crop entered intercontinental trade, it may well have been the most specialized economy in the world at that time.

Much the same kind of thing happened in the English Leeward Islands, but it started later and progressed much more slowly, partly because of insecurity during the long series of Anglo-French wars from 1680 to 1713. A colony like St. Kitts, where French planters held the two ends of the island and the English held the middle, was subject to frequent changes of European master, if only for short periods of time. But the sugar revolution came here as well, mainly in the last decades of the seventeenth century. By 1750, the Leewards were exporting three times as much sugar as Barbados, and the English Leewards had reached the stage of plantation development Barbados had reached three-quarters of a century earlier. Jamaica was still slower to develop, though its sugar industry had begun by the 1670s.

The French Antilles also lagged behind Barbados, partly because the French government still held to the idea of creating true settlement colonies. The French *engagé* went out for only three years of indenture, after which he or she became free, which may have made the status more attractive for the servant/colonists. The French flow of indented workers continued and even grew in the late seventeenth century, when the first slaves began coming in as well, and it continued well into the eighteenth century.

The 1687 census of the French Antilles tells something of what was happening. At that date, the total population was 50,000, or about the same as that of Brazil about a century earlier. Of these, 19,000 (38 percent) were from Europe, but 8,000 (16 percent) were still *engagés* working out their time. After a half-century of colonization, 42 percent of the white population had arrived only during the past three years – which gives an imperfect but impressive suggestion of the many thousands who must have been imported but soon died. The less-than-free working class also remained part-European longer than it did on the English islands. At that date, a quarter of the servants and slaves were still European.

In the next decades, however, the demographic implications of the sugar revolution worked themselves out in the French as well as the English Caribbean. By 1740, in the comparatively new colony of Saint Domingue, 82 percent of the population was slave,

8 percent was European, and the remainder were free "people of color," mostly mulattoes. As of that date, the Caribbean accounted for a sixth of the value of total French foreign and colonial trade.

Suggestions for further reading

Buffon, Alain, *Monnaie et crédit en économie coloniale: contribution a l'histoire économique de la Guadeloupe* (Basseterre: Société d'histoire de la Guadeloupe, 1979).

Debien, Gabriel, *Les esclaves aux Antilles françaises (xviie–xviiie siécles)*(Basseterre and Forte-de-France: Sociétés d'histoire de la Guadeloupe et de la Martinique, 1974).

Dunn, Richard S., *Sugar and Slaves: The Rise of the Planter Class in the English West Indies, 1624–1713* (Chapel Hill: University of North Carolina Press, 1972).

Martin, Gaston, *Histoire de l'esclavage dans les colonies françaises* (Paris: Presses Universitaires de France, 1949).

7

Anarchy and imperial control

1600

One peculiarity of the seventeenth century was the fact that the principal actors themselves shared an opaque uncertainty about the future of European activities overseas. In the sixteenth century, the main actors had been limited. In the east was the Portuguese trading post empire, designed to profit from booty or from trade, as the opportunity occurred. In the west was the Spanish empire, by the end of the century fully under Spanish government control but suffering from economic doldrums and the continuing decline of the native population. The Portuguese plantation economy in northeastern Brazil was smaller than either the true empire to the west or the trading post empire to the east.

The plantation complex had obvious weaknesses, the most obvious of which was the institution of slavery. After experimenting with Indian slavery, Spain had settled on the *encomienda* and other forms of forced labor in Spanish America. Northern Europeans did not practice slavery at home, even on the limited scale of Mediterranean Europe. Even in the Mediterranean basin, slavery was rare in agriculture, especially now that sugar planting had moved out into the Atlantic. In Brazil itself, the slave regime had the obvious weakness that deaths exceeded births, requiring a continuous supply of new labor. In retrospect, it is hard to see how such an obviously wasteful system could possibly fill any but a transitional role in American development. Yet the seventeenth century was to be a key transitional period, when the plantation complex moved on to the Caribbean and even to the southern American mainland, laying the basis for still more growth in the eighteenth and early nineteenth centuries.

86

That future could hardly have been predicted at the time. In tropical America, the seventeenth century was a period of experimentation with diverse political and economic expedients. Some of these bore fruit only briefly, if at all, whereas others gained some importance as sidelines of the plantation complex.

"No peace beyond the lines"

By the last two decades of the sixteenth century, it was apparent that the Hispanic monopoly on overseas empire could not hold much longer. More rapid economic growth in northern Europe had created competitors in Britain, France, and the Low Countries. Soon they would begin to consider where and how they could move in on the colonial world. Whatever moves the northerners made, however, would come at a peculiar juncture in European international relations.

From a very high level of generalization, the first half of the sixteenth century was dominated by the rivalry between France and Spain. By midcentury, however, France was caught up in its internal wars of religion. Sooner or later, virtually all of Europe – except Italy and the Hispanic powers – was pulled into similar wars. These religious struggles, along with a series of lucky or well-planned marriages and the wealth of the New World, created Spain's chance to try for hegemony in Europe. From the mid-1560s to the mid-1570s, indeed, it looked as though Spain would be able to dominate Europe as Napoleon and Hitler almost did at a later time.

One recurrent theme in European international relations is the "balance of power," the tendency of the smaller powers to join together in opposition to any state strong enough to threaten the independence of them all. In 1580, Philip II of Spain, who was also monarch of the Habsburg lands in central Europe and Italy, inherited the Portuguese crown as well. He could then claim control of all European empires overseas. England, France, and the Netherlands had already begun to respond to the Spanish threat, each in its own way. The northern Spanish Netherlands went into rebellion in 1568. A little later, England and France entered with their own wars against Spain, which lasted throughout the last thirty years of the century.

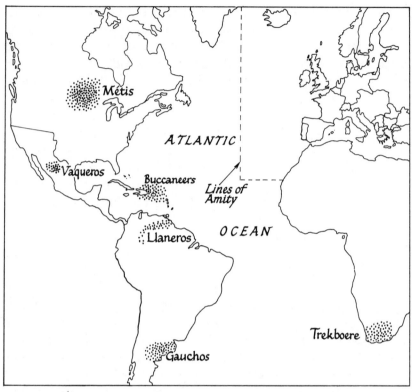

Cross-cultural groups that succeed in existance. Figure 7.1 The Atlantic Basin.

During this period, two factors were to be especially significant overseas. First, the union of the Spanish and Portuguese crowns meant that Spain's enemies could raid the wide network of Hispanic posts and colonies anywhere they chose. Second, the northern powers were relatively more powerful at sea than on land, and on land they were definitely weaker than the Habsburgs. Their most effective strategy was to avoid a frontal assault on the centers of Spanish power, concentrating instead where Spanish forces were weak and scattered. The most vulnerable targets were not only overseas, they were at the periphery of Spanish overseas power. Some attacks were semipiratical raids, like Francis Drake's expedition against Spanish South America and the East Indies. Others combined raiding with trade, trying to smuggle goods into the Spanish empire.

Then, at the turn of the century, the northern powers gradually pulled out of the war, as each found it safe enough to do so – France in 1598, England in 1604, and the Dutch in 1609 – but each signed a treaty that applied to Europe only. Neither Spain nor its enemies were apparently willing to give up the war for overseas empire. The result was the conventional "lines of amity" – an east–west line along the Tropic of Cancer to the south of the Canaries, a north–south line in the mid-Atlantic, approximately the old line of division between the Portuguese and Spanish spheres in the Americas. The treaties provided for peace in Europe but "no peace beyond the lines," and that situation lasted into the 1690s.

Where there was no peace, there was also no war, only international anarchy. This situation constituted a curious throwback to an earlier phase in the history of European international trade. In the medieval Mediterranean, relations at sea between Christians and Muslims had been those of chronic hostility. Venice and Genoa carried on their international trade as a function inseparable from maritime warfare. The Portuguese had picked up this tradition and carried it into the Indian Ocean with their earliest voyages of trade and plunder. In the Indian Ocean system of trade controls that Portugal sought to establish, no ship was free from attack unless it paid fees that were, in effect, protection money.

Meanwhile, in European waters, peace on land had come to include peace at sea. Piracy was comparatively rare; coastal shipping was comparatively safe. After the long wars of all against Spain, the convention of peaceful trade returned, but only for European waters. Beyond the lines of amity, the bellicose tradition of mixing trade and plunder, which the Portuguese had carried into the Indian Ocean, now applied to the Pacific basin and most of the Atlantic as well.

In this situation, each potential aggressor against the Hispanic empires – England, France, and the Netherlands – worked out its own strategy for using the principle of no peace beyond the lines to its advantage. The Dutch reaction was most important because the Dutch were strongest at sea. They had gradually become dominant in the northern European coastal trade. By 1594, the Dutch controlled about 60 percent of the trade from the English

Channel and the North Sea into the Baltic. Spain did little to interfere because it needed naval stores from the Baltic, and the Dutch were the only possible suppliers. The Dutch needed the profits of trade to help finance the wars. Dutch shipping therefore called at Spanish ports most of the time, in spite of the wars.

It was Philip II's closure of Spanish ports that first drove the Dutch to the Americas. The Dutch had depended heavily on Spanish salt, which was crucial for the preservation of fish and meat in the period before refrigeration. In the 1580s, when the Spanish cut off this source of supply, the Dutch began looking elsewhere, and the best source they found was a salt pan at Punta de Araya on the coast of present-day Venezuela. By the early seventeenth century, that area became a major source of salt for Europe, with an annual average of 120 Dutch ships calling there between 1599 and 1605 – along with an annual average of 25 English, 4 French, 2 Italian, 1 Scottish, and 1 Spanish ship.

The Dutch also tried to reach to or beyond other parts of the Hispanic empires. Indian Ocean trade was attractive, and the Dutch began moving in on it before the end of the sixteenth century. In the Atlantic, some advocated a frontal attack on Mexico or Peru, but others argued that land for tropical agriculture to supply raw materials and provide a market for Dutch products was easier to seize. One possibility was the neglected basin of the Rio de la Plata, the present core region of Argentina and Uruguay. Another was the "wild coast" of the Guianas between Venezuela and Brazil; Dutch Surinam ultimately grew out of that project.

In 1621, the Netherlands finally chartered a Dutch West India Company to match the Dutch East India Company already active in the Indian Ocean and the South China Sea. Like its predecessor, the new company had the authority to fight as well as trade. The Dutch thus imitated once more the combination of trade and plunder that the Portuguese had carried into the Indian Ocean. Shippers from the Low Countries had carried Madeira sugar to north European markets for many decades. Especially in the period 1609–21, the Dutch had entered the trade between Brazil and Portugal and from Portugal to northern Europe. They therefore began to learn something about tropical plantations.

The West India Company's first goal was the sugar region of

Brazil. After a pass at Bahia in 1624–5, it came back in 1630 to seize Pernambuco and the most valuable sugar lands in the northeast. The Dutch company then held northeastern Brazil until 1645 – and some parts as late as 1654. It also seized the Portuguese castles at Elmina on the Gold Coast and Luanda in Angola and held them from 1641 to 1649, providing a solid opening into the slave trade as well as the sugar trade. This combination overseas complemented the Dutch strength as carriers of low-value, high-bulk cargoes in Europe, and it opened the possibility of carrying their trading advantage into a growing plantation complex.

England had a different combination of strengths and weaknesses. English raiders sometimes reached American waters, but English maritime resources were vastly inferior to those of the Dutch. English promoters recognized that a frontal attack on part of the Spanish Empire would be risky, but they thought they saw an opportunity in regions that Spain claimed but neglected. Virginia was one – too far north for serious Spanish interest, too cold, and unoccupied. Guiana on the South American mainland was also promising, lying as it did between Spanish and Portuguese claims but occupied by neither. After 1600, English expeditions moved into Guiana, Virginia, New England, and Bermuda – all of them safely away from the forefront of the Spanish interest. It was not until the Dutch West India Company began its frontal attack after 1621 that the English dared to moved into the Caribbean, and even then they were somewhat under the Dutch shadow.

The French strategy was even more sluggish. French ships were active in the smuggling trade to Spanish America, but official French moves in North America were confined to the Saint Lawrence Valley, where they were even safer from Spanish counterattacks and where the fur trade held the promise of a profit that no one else was exploiting. Then, in the 1620s, the French moved into the Caribbean in the shadow of the Dutch. Before 1640, the French and English had occupied all of the best places for sugar in the Lesser Antilles. The Dutch, however, put their new Caribbean posts on dry islands, where opportunities for planting varied from weak to impossible – Curaçao, Sint Maarten, and Sint Eustatius, beautifully selected to serve as trade entrepôts for reaching the Spanish mainland or the rival sugar colonies.

Buccaneers and transfrontiersmen

As the European governments were moving to control the seventeenth-century Caribbean, the frontier dichotomy between slavery and anarchy arose once more as new war bands, known in this period as "buccaneers," became active. They were not simply a Caribbean oddity that flourished for a few decades. They were part of a much broader pattern of culture change on and just beyond the frontiers of European expansion – a pattern that appeared in the seventeenth century in widely scattered parts of the world. They flourished for a time, only to go under in the nineteenth century or before – suppressed and dispossessed by the forward movement of European settlement colonies.

Gathering and transporting furs was one lure calling Europeans beyond the frontier of true settlement. In North America, the French *coureurs de bois* carried the fur trade west from the Saint Lawrence Valley. In the longer run, some had to shift occupations when the supply of furbearing animals gave out. Others took Cree Indian wives, and the racial mixture gave their descendants a new identity as *métis* or *bois brulé* (as they called themselves from their skin, which had the color of scorched wood). They developed their own mixed culture and formed pockets of settlement here and there in the present-day prairie provinces, living partly from agriculture and trapping and partly from hunting buffalo. As settlers from Europe moved west, the *métis* communities came under pressure from the newcomers. Under the leadership of Louis Riel and his associates, they tried to hold on to their land, their Catholic religion, and their way of life, but they were outnumbered and overpowered. They fought the British and Canadians, however, in three sharp clashes between the 1860s and their final defeat in the 1880s.

In South Africa the *trekboere*, or seminomadic cattle and sheep farmers, also established a separate way of life from that of the sedentary settlers of the wine and wheat country around Cape Town. Their culture was partly borrowed from the African Khoi-Khoi, in much the same way that the *métis* had borrowed from the Cree. Racial mixture produced the separate communities called *bastaards* or *griquas*, who followed their own way of life under their own leaders beyond the frontier of settlement. Other *trekboere* kept their European identity, but they too tried to find refuge from European control by moving farther into the interior. Their most prominent move was the "Great Trek" of the 1840s, which led to the founding of the secondary empire of the Boer republics of the Orange Free State and the Transvaal. Some *trekboere*, however, kept going until they reached the highlands of southern Angola in the 1890s. Others tried to stand and fight it out against the imposition of Europe control – bands of *griquas* on several occasions, the burghers of the Boer republics most notably in the Anglo-Boer War at the end of the century. All were defeated, just as the *métis* had been.

In the Americas, Europeans inadvertently created transfrontier opportunities by bringing cattle and horses to the New World, where no large domestic animals had been available in pre-Columbian time. As early as the sixteenth century, pigs, goats, feral horses, and horned cattle had found an unoccupied niche and spread widely beyond the small zones of European control. Wild cattle and horses, in turn, created a new ecological niche for humans. Some Amerindians changed their way of life to take advantage of the opportunity. They passed through a "horse revolution," switching from hunting and gathering, with a little agriculture, to a nomadic way of life based horses and hunting wild cattle and bison. The horse revolution came independently in different forms and in widely dispersed places – to the Plains Indians like the Sioux and Cheyenne in North America, and to the Araucanians of southern Chile, who then spread across the Andes with their horses and cattle into the pampa of the Plata basin.

Europeans and part-Europeans on the fringes of European settlement could and did adjust to the same opportunities, sometimes just inside the frontier, sometimes beyond it. In central Mexico, the Spanish first settled as supervisors on estates worked by Indian labor, but the sedentary agricultural styles of central Mexico could not be followed in quite the same way north of the old *chichimec* frontier. In the north, dense sedentary settlement was possible on well-watered pockets of land, where irrigation was possible; otherwise, rainfall was insufficient and uncertain. But extensive pastoralism was possible, just as it was for the Indians of the Great Plains farther north. In a sense, Spanish and *mestizo* settlers in the north passed through their own horse revolution and created the pastoral way of life of the *vaquero*. Like other transfrontiersmen, the northern Mexican ranchers found themselves in recurrent conflict with the government in Mexico City – whether the viceroyalty of New Spain or the republic of Mexico. The northern ranchers' friction with the Mexican republic was less violent than that of the *métis* or the *trekboere*, but it had a place in Mexican politics as recurrent northern regionalism. It was occasionally military as well – most prominently in Francisco Villa's bid for the presidency at the head of northern troops during the civil wars of the 1910s. In the eyes of their opponents, the northern cattle people were no better than bandits, but they also stood for the values of a pastoral way of life.

By the 1920s, the central government had reestablished its control as effectively as the Canadians had done against the *métis* in Saskatchewan forty years earlier. Long before that, however, aspects of the new transfrontier *vaquero* culture had been transmiitted across national boundaries to the cowboys of the North American cattle kingdom. Some aspects can be found even today among the *paniolo* ranch hands on the island of Hawaii.

In South America, culture change beyond the frontier took place in several pastoral regions. One was the *llanos*, or plains, of the Orinoco Valley in Venezuela. Another was the *pampa* grasslands of Argentina, Uruguay, and Rio Grande do Sul in Brazil. There European or part-European transfrontiersmen saw the same opportunity as the Araucanians and adjusted their way of life accordingly. The result was the new pastoral subculture of the *gaucho*. It was different from the *vaquero* culture of Mexico, where the people merely herded cattle. The *gauchos* began as cattle hunters, just as the Canadian *métis* had been buffalo hunters. The cattle roamed free, an "open resource" in the jargon of the economists, like the fish in the sea.

Like the other transfrontiersmen, the *gauchos* founded a new culture in the seventeenth century, beyond the frontiers of settlements. In the nineteenth century, they too had to face the encroachment of an advancing frontier of sedentary settlements from Europe – private ownership of cattle, private ownership of land, and finally, barbed wire fences and wheat farming. They too fought back, principally in the first half of the century, when the civil "wars for independence" gave them a military role in

BUCCANEERS

Argentine affairs. By the 1870s, they too had been defeated and absorbed into the settlers' world.

Transfrontier cow killers also interacted with the incipient plantation complex on the Caribbean islands. In popular historiography, buccaneers are often equated with sea pirates and commerce raiders, but they began as hunters of the feral cattle and pigs on the seventeenth-century Caribbean islands. In English they were first called "cow killers," but their longer-lasting name came from the French *boucanier,* with its root *boucan,* which means to roast or dry meat over an open fire.

The ecological conditions that made their way of life possible grew out of the post-Columbian exchange of diseases and cultigens. European diseases decimated the Caribbean populations, and the European cattle, gone wild on the islands, were there for the taking. The political condition that made buccaneering possible in its piratical sense was the principle of no peace beyond the lines. No peace, no war – and no law. European cow killers could then operate outside the framework of the national state system – a voluntary community of stateless persons.

A further factor was the presence of uprooted people. Sailors were sometimes put on shore or mutinied against their officers. Indented servants sometimes escaped from the early European plantations or were replaced by African slaves as the plantation complex took over the economy of one island after another. Some of the white servants on Barbados or the French islands went home again or moved to the mainland colonies in North America, but many who had no capital drifted off to other parts of the Caribbean, where cattle killing and banditry were open pursuits.

The Greater Antilles were theoretically Spanish, but the Spanish found it hard to protect anything but their main towns. A force from England conquered the island of Jamaica between 1655 and 1660. The western end of the island of Hispaniola – the future Haiti – was even more open. It was easy enough for buccaneers to move into the back country or onto a small island, living on the meat of the wild cattle, selling the hides and dried meat to passing ships, and occasionally taking hides and salt meat to ports where the sugar economy was fully established. Many who settled on western Hispaniola were French, but other nationalities were also present.

Though their numbers were never large, the cow killers

emerged as a group of men with skills that made them effective raiders. At their height in the 1660s, the buccaneers of all nationalities may have numbered as many as 10,000 – including cattle killers who did nothing else, as well as active fighters. The transition to raiding came in the 1670s and lasted up to the mid 1680s. In 1670, one force, mainly English, organized by Henry Morgan and patronized by the English governor of Jamaica, marched across the Isthmus of Panama to capture and burn Panama City on the Pacific coast. French buccaneer raids also sought Spanish prizes, and in 1683 a Franco-Dutch buccaneer force attacked and captured Vera Cruz, the principal port for highland Mexico. Many French bucacaneers gathered in the western part of Hispaniola, beyond the control of the Spanish government in Santo Domingo. By the 1680s, theirs was the de facto government of the region, which made possible a relatively peaceful transfer to the French state in 1697 – the foundation of the French colony of Saint Domingue, the most valuable of the French sugar colonies.

After the 1680s, with the reestablishment of worldwide peace between the European states, the buccaneers found it hard to continue. Many died, and no one came to take their place. Many moved into other occupations. Some were bought off by European governments or enlisted in the official armed forces. European states found them no more useful than they were to find other transfrontiersmen once the period of anarchy had passed. In the Caribbean after the 1680s, some commerce raiding still occurred, but such raiding by private individuals was now defined as piracy. It persisted through the eighteenth century as a violent background to international warfare, but in the Caribbean as a whole, anarchy gave way to slavery. The last Caribbean pirate was hanged in the 1830s, the decade that brought emancipation to the British islands.

Suggestions for further reading

Crosby, Alfred W., *The Columbian Exchange: Biological and Cultural Consequences of 1492* (Westport, Conn: Greenwood Press, 1972).

Haring, C. H., *The Buccaneers in the West Indies in the Seventeenth Century* (London: Methuen, 1910).

Howard, Joseph Kinsey, *Strange Empire: A Narrative of the Northwest* (Westport, Conn: Greenwood Press, 1974).

Knight, Franklin W., *The Caribbean: The Genesis of a Fragmented Nationalism* (London: Oxford University Press, 1978).

Parry, John H., Philip Sherlock, and Anthony Maingot, *A Short History of the West Indies*, 4th ed. (New York: St. Martin's Press, 1987).

Slatta, Richard W., *Gauchos and the Vanishing Frontier* (Lincoln: University of Nebraska Press, 1983).

Sluiter, Engel, "Dutch–Spanish Rivalry in the Caribbean Area, 1594–1609," *Hispanic-American Historical Review*, 28:165–96 (1948).

Thompson, Alvin, *Colonialism and Underdevelopment in Guyana, 1580–1803* (Bridgetown, Barbados: Caribbean Research and Publications, 1987).

8

Slave societies on the periphery

The Atlantic slave trade was central to the plantation complex, but it delivered labor for other pruposes as well. In the Americas generally, the death of the Indians meant that all economic development needed imported labor – whether in the true-colony sector of North America or the true-empire sector of the highlands from Mexico south to Chile. The influx of slave labor was so great that it was not until the 1840s that more Europeans than Africans crossed the Atlantic to populate the New World.

Differential population growth

New World populations of European descent were nevertheless comparatively large, and those from Africa were comparatively small. The difference came from differential rates of population growth. As we have seen, people from Africa survived better than people from Europe did in the tropical lowlands, but elsewhere in the Americas, populations from Europe thrived. In general, these settler populations in the New World tended to increase even more rapidly than the population of Europe itself.

The usual explanation is that the standard of living was higher for the settlers than it was for those who stayed at home, which was no doubt the case; but the evidence of historical epidemiology in the nineteenth century suggests that biological factors may also have been present. In the worldwide spread of disease, the Americas, Australasia, and some of the Pacific islands were comparatively isolated. Their people lacked the immunities of the greater intercommunicating zone, and hence died of disease on contact with outsiders. But their isolation may also have made them less dangerous to Europeans than Europe itself would have been.

Nineteenth-century data on disease and mortality among European soldiers overseas show that their death rates were almost always higher than those of soldiers who served in Europe, with only a few exceptions. Those exceptions were New Zealand, New Caledonia, Hawaii, and Tahiti – all of them isolated, all of them free of malaria, yellow fever, and cholera (among the main tropical killers). All were in the isolated zone, with minimal immunity against the diseases that the Europeans brought in. The entering Europeans, furthermore, had lower-than-European death rates from some of the very diseases that carried off the native populations – especially tuberculosis, pneumonia, and smallpox.

For the Americas, we lack similar medical evidence for the first centuries after contact with Europe, but the nineteenth-century evidence may reflect conditions that prevailed in earlier centuries as well. British troops in Canada, for example, were a little healthier than those who served at home. The situation in the West Indies was even more striking. The disease death rates for European soldiers there were among the highest in the world, but if deaths from malaria and yellow fever are set aside, European troops there were healthier than those who stayed in Britain. And their lower death rates were from precisely the diseases that spared other soldiers in the Pacific basin – tuberculosis, pneumonia, and smallpox. If similar conditions had been true of highland South America in earlier centuries, the Europeans there might have profited from the epidemiological isolation that was so disastrous to the local people.[1]

Whatever the cause, the European population grew rapidly in the tropical highlands and in North America. Even the Indian populations began to increase in the eighteenth century, but the African-derived and most of the European-derived populations of the plantation complex kept their net natural decrease until the end of slavery. Since the plantation sector required a steady

[1] Philip D. Curtin, *Death by Migration: The European Encounter with the Tropics in the Nineteenth Century* (New York: Cambridge University Press, 1989).

supply of labor from abroad, it was only natural for the others to draw on that supply.

Placer gold

The Spanish territorial empires had drawn in African populations even before the plantation complex appeared, and they continued to do so. Africans participated in the conquest of Mexico and in every expedition to Peru. By the middle of the sixteenth century there were more Afro-Americans than Euro-Americans in coastal Peru, just as there were more Afro-Americans than Euro-Americans in Mexico toward the end of the sixteenth century. In 1545, for the first time on record in the New World, escaped slaves tried to set up an African kingdom in Peru.

Most of the Africans who arrived in the Spanish Empire during its first decades were slaves, but they were domestics, craftsmen, and skilled servants of several kinds, rarely agricultural workers. Most came by way of Spain, not directly from Africa. Many of these sixteenth-century slaves succeeded in gaining their freedom after a time. Some rose in colonial society. Toward the middle of the sixteenth century, one freed African in what was to be Chile became an *encomendero*, authorized to collect labor and other tribute from the defeated Amerindians in return for military service to the Spanish crown. Even the pastoral transfrontier populations of *gauchos* and *llaneros* attracted large numbers of Afro-Americans escaped from the plantation complex, and Afro-Americans figured among the *vaqueros* of northern Mexico, as they did among the North American cowboys. The sectors of American development – like true empire, true colony, and transfrontier cultures – were quite distinct, but the importance of the slave trade as a source of population was so great that Africans found their way into all of them.

Most slaves who moved into the true-empire sector, however, were miners. As the Indians died out, the labor shortage in the mines became serious. In Upper Peru (now Bolivia), the need for slave labor was so great toward the end of the sixteenth century that a regular slave trade ran from the Atlantic coast near Buenos Aires, where the slaves were formed into caravans and walked overland across the *pampa* and into the Peruvian highlands. The

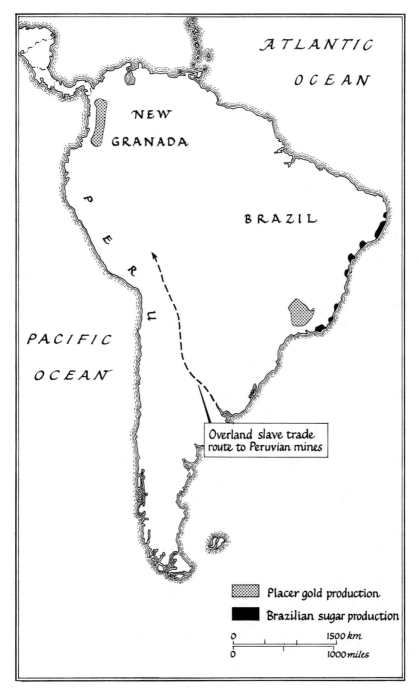

ATLANTIC

OCEAN

NEW
GRANADA

P
E
R
U

BRAZIL

PACIFIC

OCEAN

Overland slave trade
route to Peruvian mines

Placer gold production
Brazilian sugar production

0   1500 km
0   1000 miles

Fgure 8.1 South American gold and sugar regions.

Pacific coast, however, was far from the main line of entry by Africans into the Americas.

Many more slaves came into the Spanish Empire from the Caribbean coasts, where again they were used in mining labor. This was especially so in the western part of Nueva Granada, the present-day Colombia, where placer gold mining was important in the eighteenth century. Here the pattern of plantation demography tended to reassert itself; births were fewer than deaths, and the mining industry consumed slaves just as the plantations did.

Placer mining was even more important in Brazil. In the 1690s, gold strikes in Minas Gerais, the hinterland of central Brazil, set off a gold rush that made Brazil rich once more, and the gold prosperity ran through the first half of the eighteenth century. In the longer run, Brazil was to furnish Europe with more gold than Mexico and Peru had done. Many of the Europeans who came for gold came from the sugar regions of northeastern Brazil. They came with habits and knowledge of the institutions formed in the sugar region. Brazilian gold mining was thus an adaptation to the mining industry of the patterns first created for tropical agriculture.

The gold, and later diamonds, were dug by slaves – 90,000 to 100,000 of them working at any time in the early eighteenth century. Thus, far more slaves worked the mines than had worked sugar at the height of the sugar prosperity early in the seventeenth century. Population figures for colonial Brazil are notoriously bad, but it would be reasonable to guess that the number of slaves in mining about 1735 was not very different from the number of plantation slaves. It is also safe to guess that, over the whole period of slavery, at least as many African slaves were imported to work the gold fields of Minas Gerias as were imported into the United States.

Bandeirantes

Another group of transfrontiersmen related to the plantation complex were the *bandeirantes* of São Paulo. It began to take form in the late sixteenth century, when European settlers moved to a region that was then the frontier between Portuguese America and the uncontrolled Indian territory of the central plateau of Brazil. In this setting, and with a scarcity of Portuguese women, race mixture took place between Europeans and Tupí Indians, similar to that of the métis of western Canada. These early Paulistas began to participate in the Indian trade of the interior. They called themselves Portuguese, and they were in some respects, though most seem to have used Tupí as their home language. Then, especially in the early seventeenth century, they switched from being mainly traders to being mainly raiders among the Indians, catching slaves for the sugar plantations of the northeast.

Military units formed for a raid were called *bandeiras,* hence *bandeirantes* as a generic term for the participants. The *bandeirante* operations were curiously like those the buccaneers in that these groups too were raiders and war bands, though the *bandeirantes* raided overland. As with the buccaneers, one of their favorite targets was Spanish America, in this case the string of Indian settlements formed by Jesuit missionaires in Paraguay. The Jesuits had persuaded certain Amerindian hunting groups to settle down as Christian farmers. These settlements in concentrated villages made them an easy target for the Paulista slave raiders.

The timing of the *bandeirante* activities was similar to that of the buccaneers. They were most successful in the period of the Dutch occupation of the northeast, no doubt because the Portuguese part of Brazil was no longer able to import slaves from Africa as easily as it had once done. The Paulista raids seem to have increased in intensity until about the 1650s, after which they gradually declined through the rest of the century. Nor were these raids a minor source of labor supply. The most frequently cited estimate claims that the *bandeirantes* brought in about 350,000 slaves during the sixteenth and seventeenth centuries. If true, this would mean that nearly one-third of the slaves entering the Brazilian economy in those two centuries were the product of Paulista raids – the other two-thirds being from Africa. In the eighteenth century and later, Paulistas still wandered widely in the interior, usually trading or prospecting for gold and diamonds rather than raiding for slaves, as they had done in the seventeenth.

Slave revolts and maroon settlements

Africans who escaped from the plantation complex sometimes formed offshoot communities in the vicinity. One historical myth about African slavery in the New World was the belief that the slaves were docile. In fact, they were far from docile, and large concentrations of slaves on a single plantation opened the possibility of a concerted revolt.

Revolts on tropical plantations can be divided into three types. First were the revolts of despair or last resort – without any long-run plans or possibilities. For some, the goal was revenge against the master or his associates. Milder disturbances were protests against a specific grievance. A second category of revolts aimed to seize control of the country or region. This class was rare, and the odds against success were very high. Slaves rarely had access to arms, and they had little experience with the large-scale organization needed to bring off such a revolt – much less to keep it going over any length of time. The final major possibility was to run away. In North America, escaped slaves could try to get to Canada. No such refuge existed in the tropics – except to make for the back country. There, it was often possible to defend a small territorial enclave against the Europeans' effort at conquest and reenslavement. In the Caribbean, these independent Africans were called "maroons," from the Spanish *cimarrones*, or people from the heights, and maroon settlements existed on every sizable Caribbean island. Unfortunately, we know much less about these settlements than we might like; they made it their business to keep a low profile, though a few left some indirect data for the historical record. Several maroon settlements held out long enough to arrive at a formal or informal understanding with the plantation authorities.

Maroon colonies on Jamaica already existed before the English invasion of 1655, and the English authorities left them alone at first. Later, in the early eighteenth century, the Jamaican government sent out a number of military expeditions against them, with varying success. It finally settled down to accommodation and signed a series of treaties recognizing the maroons' rights to certain territory. In return, the maroons promised to help fight slave rebellions on the plantations themselves. New wars between the government and the maroons nevertheless broke out from time to time. In the 1790s, the island authorities managed to break up the largest of the settlements, sending the defeated into exile in Nova Scotia and then to Sierra Leone, but they continued to recognize the maroon identity in other settlements. Some settlements, indeed, have kept that identity and some of their separate cultural heritage down to the present.

The most successful marronage of all was to obtain such a secure charter of freedom that it was no longer necessary to live in the back country. One well-documented case from sixteenth-century Mexico describes a maroon settlement that first defended itself, then obtained a treaty, and finally gained enough security to move into colonial society as free men and women. In time, the community of free African-Americans in any plantation society tended to grow through manumission until it constituted a subgroup within colonial society capable of absorbing ex-maroons who might not be detected. In Brazil in particular, by the early nineteenth century, individuals sometimes circulated between the free black communities of the cities and the maroon settlements nearby.

The most impressive and successful maroon colonies were on the mainland rather than the islands. They existed from time to time almost everywhere in Spanish and Portuguese America with a hinterland into which slaves could flee – in the Guianas, in Mexico, and, most impressively of all, on the Pacific coastal plains of Colombia and Ecuador. There, slaves escaping from the placer gold workings in highland Colombia made their way over the mountains and onto the coastal plains, were they then migrated south over the decades into Ecuador. For long periods, highland colonial governments knew they were there but made no serious effort to administer their territory. Their neighbors included a number of Amerindian groups that were also allowed to go their own way. Many of these African communities maintained their independence far into the nineteenth century, though slavery was long since abolished and they were free to join the national society if they wanted to do so. Many, no doubt, did migrate to coastal towns like Buenaventura in Colombia and Esmeraldas or Guayaquil in Ecuador.

Another center of maroon settlements was northeastern Brazil, where they were called *quilombos*, from the African *kilombo*, a war camp in several western Bantu languages spoken in the Congo Republic, Zaïre, and Angola. We know little about most of these, beyond the fact that such settlements existed most of the time from the late sixteenth century into the nineteenth. Many were villages, organized as they were in Africa, but without a political structure above the village level. Others were more nearly fugitive camps, like those in the mountains around Rio de Janeiro in the nineteenth century.

At least one real kingdom, called Palmares, came into existence at an uncertain date in the second half of the sixteenth century. It lasted until 1694 – and even later for some of its inhabitants, who escaped to other *quilombos* farther inland. The name itself is obviously Portuguese, not African. Unlike many *quilombos*, Palmares was not hidden in the mountains; it held good agricultural land bordering the plantation complex itself. It finally fell, but only to a major military expedition. The kingdom's boundaries changed from time to time according to the fortunes of war, but the center was the town of Macaco, later the Brazilian city of União, in the hinterland of Pernambuco about seventy miles from that city and about twenty-five miles from the coast. Some recent maps show União as Palmares.

Its political organization followed an African pattern, like that of the Ambunbu people from the hinterland of Luanda in Angola. This is hardly unexpected, since the area around the Congo's mouth was the principal source of Brazilian slaves both then and later. In any event, the African tradition continued to change in the New World – like that of any other culture. Palmares was theoretically Christian, though it also continued to practice some aspects of the lower Congo religion. The people lived mainly in villages, each of them under a village chief responsible to the king in Macaco. The king, in turn, was drawn from a royal lineage and ruled with the advice and consent of a council.

The main economic activity was agriculture, in which African subsistence crops, American crops like maize and manioc, and some sugarcane were grown. The people of the *quilombo* also practiced blacksmithing, as their ancestors in Africa had done. They made their own gunpowder, and they occasionally made firearms by hand. Most of their arms, however, and most of the iron they used to make tools were captured from the plantations.

Palmares's military operations were not merely defensive. It too was a slaveholding society, and raids against the Portuguese were one way of keeping up and increasing their numbers. The main towns, both Macaco and smaller centers, were fortified with elaborate log stockades, which made them relatively safe against anything short of a large-scale attack with artillery.

The *quilombo's* relations with surrounding plantations, however, were not necessarily those of permanent warfare. The rulers occasionally signed agreements not to raid the plantations, and they sometimes received tribute from the plantations in the form of rent or protection money. Their attitude toward Africans still enslaved on the Portuguese plantations was to consider them free if they escaped and found their way to Palmares. If, on the other hand, they were captured in the course of a raid, they were still considered slaves and joined the slave class in the *quilombo* itself – though we may assume that this was an African form of domestic slavery, not plantation slavery on the European model.

The size of Palmares's population must have fluctuated a good deal, depending on the success of the various Portuguese and Dutch attempts to wipe it out. Portuguese and Dutch visitors estimated the size of Macaco at about 5,000 to 15,000, with the lower figure more likely. A city in the upper range would have been large for contemporary Angola or for a Portuguese provincial city, though the kingdom's territory near the height of its powers would have supported a much larger population. It stretched for about 130 miles parallel to the coast and just back from the coastal plain, and it reached about 100 miles into the interior.

Once the Dutch threat to Portuguese Brazil disappeared after the mid-1650s, the Brazilian government was in a position to take firmer action, though the threat became serious only in the 1670s. From 1675 to 1687, Brazil sent military expeditions, mainly to capture territory around the fringes of Palmares, so that the core of the kingdom was not yet threatened. From 1692 to 1694, however, the government mounted a large-scale offensive, calling for troops from all over Brazil to assemble a total force of some 3,000 men equipped with artillery. An army of that size was remarkable for its time and place. It was comparable to the armies the Portuguese had used against the Dutch in their struggle for northeastern Brazil.

Palmares was best known because of its location near the coast, which means that it was most threatening to the Europeans. Some of the other maroon settlements that managed to keep quiet also managed to survive. Some of those on the coastal plains of western Equador were effectively free of Equadorian control from Quito into the early twentieth century.

The settlement colonies

Some of the more ethnocentric versions of U.S. history imply that the American South was the heart of the plantation sector in the New World. That was not the case. The mainland colonies bought a few slaves in the seventeenth century, who were usually assimilated to the status of indented servants. It was only from the early eighteenth century on that slave plantations became characteristic of the American South, after the sugar revolution had already moved to the Greater Antilles. When plantation slavery did come, it copied from the British West Indies, just as the Lesser Antilles had earlier copied Brazil.

Even then, the American South was not fully part of the plantation complex. In the typical sugar islands, 75 to 95 percent of the population were slaves, and many of the free people were either mulatto or black. In the American South generally, most people were not slaves at all, but colonists of European descent. Even where, as in South Carolina, a majority of the working class were slaves, they worked alongside a Euro-American working class that was free.

The American South also differed from the heart of the plantation complex in work organization and plantation size. The typical Caribbean sugar plantation had at least 50 slaves – more often 200 or even 300. In the United States, even in the 1850s, when slavery reached its fullest development, fewer than half of the slaves belonged to planters who owned 30 or more. Gang labor, where dozens of men and women worked side by side under constant disciplinary surveillance, was most typcial of sugar cultivation. The more diversified plantations of the American South often grew specialized export crops like cotton and tobacco, but they also grew food for themselves and for the rest of society. Raising pigs, cattle, and chickens, as well as field crops, created too great a variety of tasks for continuous supervision.

The demographic history of the American South was also

strikingly different from that of the tropical plantation colonies. In the tropics, slave populations experienced an excess of deaths over births from their earliest settlement on. European populations of the tropical Caribbean also had more deaths than births. Both had to be renewed by continuous immigration from Europe and Africa. In North America, on the other hand, the slave population soon began to grow from natural increase, and the population of free settlers from Europe grew even more rapidly. Further migration from Europe and Africa simply increased the total. It is not yet possible to account for this striking difference. Part of the explanation must be found in the healthier environment of a country with winter frosts to kill off some tropical diseases, but the American South had malaria and occasional yellow fever epidemics. Part may be the American achievement of a more even sex ratio in the slave population at an early date, which, in turn, may reflect the greater variety of tasks and the smaller size of the American slave plantation.

In any event, both Afro-American and Euro-American populations in the mainland colonies grew from natural increase, and they increased more rapidly than contemporaneous populations did in Europe. As a result, the United States is thought to have the largest population of partial or total African descent in any country in the Americas – about 30 percent of all Afro-Americans in the New World – even though their African ancestors made up only about 6 percent of the total slave trade.

Though the number of African-born in each North American generation was compartively small, our African ancestors arrived a good deal earlier than our European ancestors did. The median date of arrival for the ancestors of present-day Afro-Americans was about 1770 – half, that is, arrived before that date and half arrived later. The equivalent median date for the arrival of Euro-Americans was about 1900.

This compartively early arrival also made an enormous difference in the history of African culture in the United States. Though many Euro-Americans have talked to a grandfather or grandmother who was born in Europe, this is simply not possible for most Afro-Americans, other than those descended from the new African immigrants who began to arrive in the 1950s. It is sometimes said that the passage through slavery muted the survival of African culture. That may be, but the passage of time muted it even more. Marked survivals of African culture are less frequent among black Americans than they are among Afro-Cubans, some of whom could still speak Yoruba in the 1980s. By the same token, the remnants of African culture that did survive in the United States came to be very widely diffused, especially in the South. Cultural traits of African origin can be found in the white community, as well as the black, and in new forms that have continued to evolve in the United States – forms as various as jazz, southern cooking, and expected behavior in church.

To say this is not to play down the importance of African culture in the United States or the importance of slave plantations in the history of the American South. They were obviously crucial to the development of the southern economy, of southern society, and of the regional differences that helped to bring on the American Civil War. But in the broader perspective of the plantation complex, the plantation regime of the American South was a curiously atypical and late-flowering institution that reached its peak between the 1820s and the 1850s, when may plantations societies in the Caribbean were already in dissolution.

Suggestions for further reading

Carroll, Patrick J., "Mandinga: The Evolution of a Mexican Runaway Slave Community, 1735–1827," *Comparative Studies in Society and History,*19: 488–505 (1977).

Heumans, Gad (ed.), *Out of the House of Bondage: Runaways, Resistance and Marronage in Africa and the New World* (London: Frank Cass, 1986).

Karasch, Mary, *Slave Life in Rio de Janeiro, 1808–1850* (Princeton: Princeton University Press, 1986).

Kent, Raymond K., "Palmares: An African State in Brazil," *Journal of African History*, 6:161–75 (1965).

Morris, Richard M., *The Bandeirantes: The Historical Role of Brazilian Pathfinders* (New York: Alfred A. Knopf, 1965).

Rubin, Vera, and Arthur Tuden (eds.), *Compartive Persepctives on Slavery in New World Societies* (New York: New York Acadmey of Sciences, 1977).

Russell-Wood, A.J.R., *The Black Man in Slavery and Freedom in Colonial Brazil* (London: Macmillan, 1982).

Apogee and revolution

9

The slave trade and the West African economy in the eighteenth century

For twentieth-century North Americans, the Atlantic slave trade is hard to put in perspective. More Americans trace their ancestors to Africa than to any continent other than Europe, and it was the slave trade that brought them; but that phase of our past carries strong emotional overtones – for Afro-Americans and Euro-Americans alike. These feelings involve guilt, shame, and the attempt to assess blame for atrocities committed by people long since dead.

No one today defends the slave trade as a humane institution, and few indeed defend it on any grounds. It may be well to concede that the era of the slave trade is beyond the effective range of moral condemnation – and to try to find out what happened and why, rather than placing blame, however well deserved. The Atlantic slave trade grew to be the largest intercontinental migration up to its time. One way to begin is to see the trade as an economic enterprise.

Prices

Whatever else, the slave trade existed because West Indian, Brazilian, and other New World planters were willing and able to pay for them. The tropical American lowlands had been denuded of population, and economic development of any kind needed people. In the circumstances of the sixteenth, seventeenth, and eighteenth centuries, that population had to come from somewhere else, and that meant, in the first instance, either Europe, Africa, or American regions away from the plantation zone. All three of these sources was tapped, but Africa supplied the most people. Asia was still too far away and too expensive to reach, though Asian labor was called on in the nineteenth century.

In addition to external labor sources, another alternative was available, though contemporaries rarely considered it or even knew that it existed. That alternative was simply to wait. With time, the native-born population would acquire the immunities suited to the local disease environment. Immigrants lacked these immunities. Paradoxically, strong economic growth brought immigrants from Africa and Europe, and the newcomers' death rates – often 40 to 150 per 1,000 – were higher than any birth rates that might be expected, even in the best circumstances. Economic stagnation, on the other hand, allowed the children and grand-children of immigrants to adjust to the new disease environment. Countries with only minimal continued immigration could develop natural growth. This was true of the colored or racially mixed segment in any planting society, who were native born almost by definition. By the eighteenth century, this had become the case for all racial groups in economic backwaters like Cuba, Puerto Rico, or Spanish Santo Domingo. A plantation society willing to accept this slow natural increase could have avoided the slave trade, with its high mortality for all concerned.

Planters were impatient, however, and not merely because they wanted to expand production. They also knew, or thought they knew, that the price of slaves imported from Africa was even lower than the cost of supporting a child from birth to the age of about fourteen, when he or she could begin a normal working life. This belief was virtually universal among planters in Brazil and the Caribbean throughout the first half of the eighteenth century, and sometimes even later. After about the 1760s, however, some West Indian planters began to change their minds. As they looked at the rising prices they had to pay for new hands (see Figure 9.1),[1] they began trying to reduce miscarriages and infant mortality among the slaves they already owned. Better medical care, time off during the late months of pregnancy, time off for nursing mothers, and occasional rewards for mothers of several children were all means to this end.

[1] For numerical equivalents, see Appendix Table 1.

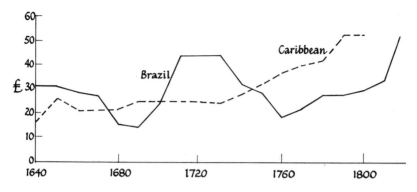

Figure 9.1 Slave prices in Brazil and the Caribbean from the 1620s to the 1820s.

The price of slaves in the Americas varied considerably from place to place. Figure 9.1 compares prices in Brazil and the West Indies. The Brazilian prices were more variable, and they moved in response to Brazilian demand rather than to supply in Africa. The chart thus shows the phases of Brazilian prosperity. In the middle decades of the seventeenth century, prices were high, and they continued to be high until Brazilian sugar began to face important Caribbean competition. From 1700 on, however, they rose again, even more steeply, in accord with the gold boom in Minas Gerais, only to fall off once more as the gold ran out. The final dramatic rise, from about 1800 to the 1830s, was based on coffee in São Paulo, with some help from a new sugar industry in coastal Rio de Janeiro. The price of slaves in the West Indies, on the other hand, remained fairly steady until the 1750s. It then began to rise until it had more than doubled by the 1790s.

New demand for slaves led to higher prices for slaves in Africa as well, and there prices rose even more rapidly (Figure 9.2).[2] In Luanda, the principal slave market of Angola, the price of slaves rose more than fourfold between the 1700s and the 1820s, whereas the selling price in Brazil slightly more than doubled. On the coast of Senegal, slave prices rose even faster, whereas the Caribbean selling price again slightly more than doubled. If the African price

[2] For numerical equivalents, see Appendix Table 2.

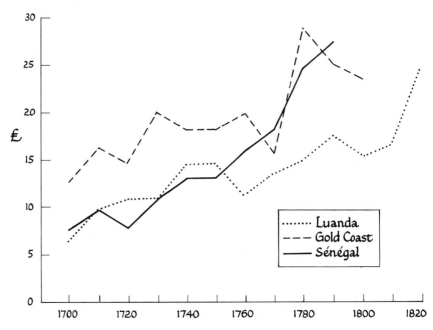

Figure 9.2 Slave prices in Africa from the 1700s to the 1820s.

changes were merely a reflection of the American prices, one might expect a narrowing difference between the African and American prices brought about by the improving efficiency and decreasing costs of ocean shipping throughout the eighteenth century. Instead, the Europeans were forced to pay more and more European goods for the slaves they bought, and the gap between American and African prices widened.

The economics of supply

In the Americas, this increase in the price of slaves encouraged planters to substitute population growth for importation from abroad, but its consequences in Africa were much more diverse. One underlying condition was the cheapness of slaves in Africa. The West Indian planters thought that it was cheaper to buy workers from Africa than it was to produce them locally, which implied that African slave dealers could sell a slave for less than it cost to bring up a child to working age. But how could Africans sell people for less than their cost of production?

The local economic situation at the mouth of the Gambia River in the 1680s may illustrate part of this underlying condition. At that time, a young male slave ready for shipment sold for an assortment of goods that cost about £5.50 sterling in Europe. Five pounds sterling at that time would have bought 17 trade muskets or 200 liters of brandy or 349 kilograms of wrought iron. Even at that time of comparatively low prices, these were no mere trinkets, but their value may be clearer when translated into local terms. One way to give such prices an approximate local value is to find their equivalent in important foods. The most important food cost is that of the local starchy staple, with daily consumption estimated at one kilogram per person. Man does not live by millet alone, nor was anyone likely to eat quite that much millet every day, but the index can serve as a rough guide to the cost of one person's subsistence. For the Gambia of the 1680s, the price of a slave, f. o. b., could buy enough food to support him or her for about six years. It was therefore much less than the probable cost of raising a child to working age. But the selling price on the coast was far more than the value of the slave at the point of enslavement. European slave dealers resident on the coast bought slaves from African dealers for only about £3.40, the difference being their profit, along with the cost of holding slaves until a ship happened along. The African merchants who brought slaves for sale to the European post paid, in turn, less still – prices ranging from about £3.00 for a slave purchased near the port to £1.00 or less for slaves bought in the distant interior. The difference was the cost of tolls and transportation on the way to the coast. At these approximate prices, the original enslaver got the value of about four years of support costs near the coast down to barely a year's support in the interior.

Such a price was obviously lower than the slave's cost of production, but the first seller was not the producer. The economic model for enslavement is a burglary model, not a production model. In economic terms, the value of the slave is not a real cost but an "opportunity cost."

Returning to the hypothetical example from the Gambia of the

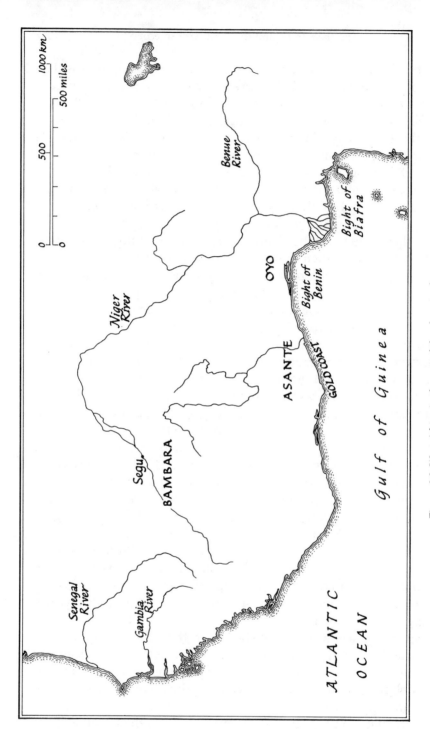

Figure 9.3 West Africa in the era of the slave trade.

1680s, we can imagine a king of Segu on the upper Niger fighting one of his brothers for control of the kingdom. If, in the process, he captured one of his brother's villages, he was entitled by law and custom to enslave the inhabitants. Since he was fighting a war for other reasons, the captives were essentially costless to the king, but the opportunity cost was also low. One possibility was to keep the slaves as an addition to the labor force under his command, but recent enemies of fighting age were dangerous unless they could be kept under constant guard, and few African societies were prepared to run the equivalent of a chain gang. To try might have been uneconomical in any case; the cost of food and guards might well exceed the value of labor performed unwillingly. The usual practice was therefore to sell a slave into the trade for transportation to a distant point, whence individual captives had small chance of getting home alone. The new owner could then try to assimilate them into a new society.

Political enslavement

Political enslavement occurred when economic motives for enslavement were secondary, though not necessarily absent, as in the example just given. Enslavement of this kind belongs near one end of a spectrum of motives ranging from the purely political at one end to the purely economic at the other – from enslavement in the pursuit of power to enslavement in the pursuit of wealth. At the extreme political end of the spectrum, captives were not sold at all but killed on the spot. At the economic end, the captors acted solely for material gain.

Large-scale enslavement mainly for political motives arose from civil wars like that of Segu in the 1680s, from international wars of aggression, or from civil disorder following the collapse of a large state. When these disturbances took place, they often caused a major increase in the supply of slaves from that particular region – a change that had little or nothing to do with the price offered on the coast. In the case of the upper Niger, a new, mainly Bambara kingdom based on Segu was formed in the early eighteenth century. From about 1700 to 1730, unusual numbers of slaves were sold down the trade routes toward the Senegambian coastal ports. Once the new dynasty was firmly in control, the price of slaves began its eighteenth-century rise, but the flow of slaves from Segu dropped to a trickle, and the slavers went elsewhere.

The political expansion of the kingdom of Asante was one of several cases of imperial expansion in eighteenth-century West Africa. The new state was first firmly established in the Gold Coast hinterland in about 1700. It then proceeded to fight a series of wars of aggression, first against neighboring states of the same Akan ethnic group and later against its neighbors to the north. In later years, the Asante also fought rebellions in subject states that were unhappy about their subordination to Asante power. With each outbreak, new flows of slaves entered the trade to the coast. The supply of slaves on the Gold Coast rose and fell with these known events of Asante military history, not with changes in the price offered.

A third example was the early-nineteenth-century collapse of the formerly powerful Oyo empire in southwestern Nigeria. Oyo had established a broad region of hegemony over the densely inhabited Yoruba city-states and many of their neighbors. During the height of Oyo power, comparatively few Oyo entered the slave trade. When the empire collapsed, however, a half-century of warfare followed among the successor states, with the result that the Yoruba, who had been rare in the eighteenth-century slave trade, became the largest single ethnic group in the nineteenth century trade. As a result, New World countries that imported many slaves in the nineteenth century – Brazil and Cuba in particular – received an unusual concentration of Yoruba and an overlay of Yoruba culture that has persisted to the present.

A final example is not one of political enslavement in the sense of the other three examples, but another case where slaves found their way into the trade for reasons other than economic demand. Tropical Africa is a region of notoriously variable rainfall, especially in the sahel region in West Africa just south of the Sahara and in equivalent regions in Angola south of the equator. These savanna areas north or south of the equator have a restricted period of rainfall in any case, and the entire year's rainfall occurs in a period of two to four months. When such intense rainfall is badly distributed throughout the growing season, crop failure and famine can result. Worse still, rain sometimes fails altogether for

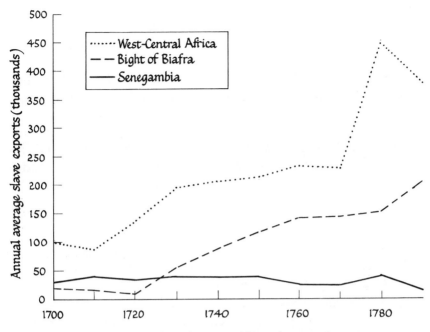

Figure 9.4 Eighteenth-century African slave exports.

a whole season – and occasioanlly for two or even three years in succession. When that happened, people either had to flee or die.

Those who fled were easy victims for the slave trade. Some sold themsleves or family members in order to survive. Others had to take refuge with alien societies, which they entered as kinless people with no rights. As such, they were easily transferred to the slave trade whenever their hosts wished to do so. It is not always possible to distinguish famine victims from other slaves, but a few instances were dramatic enough to come to the attention of Europeans on the coast. Between 1746 and 1754, Senegal experienced a series of bad harvests, which brought measurable increases in slave exports. Even though the general level of the Senegalese slave trade had been falling for decades, French exports from the Senegal in 1754 were the highest ever.

The impact of low rainfall is even more striking in Angola, where a severe famine struck in the 1780s, continuing into the

1790s (see Figure 9.4). In the 1780s, slave exports from West-
Central Africa, where Angola was located, jumped to twice the
level of the 1770s – even though the price rose from one decade
to the next by only 10 percent. Though the region had once been
a source of supply only for Portuguese slavers, French, British, and
Dutch slave traders now began operating on the coast north of the
Congo mouth. These political and climatic disasters were non-
economic in origin, but they had the economic consequence of
lowering the price of slaves as they flooded the nearby coastal
areas and attracting new groups of maritime slave traders ready
to supply the markets of the plantation complex.

Economic enslavement

Economic enslavement can take many forms; the most obvious is
a war started purely for the sake of booty. European accounts of
precolonial Africa feature the "slave-raiding chief" as a stock
figure. Whether, or how often, wars were begun for the sole
purpose of capturing slaves is hard to establish. Before the
eighteenth-century rise in slave prices, the captor's share of the
total price was too low to justify any considerable risk to himself
– or to his cavalry horses, which were worth many times the price
of a slave. As the coastal price of slaves rose throughout the
eighteenth century, however, rulers took these prices into account
in making decisions – along with whatever nonmaterial advantage was also present.

The state, however, could recruit slaves in less risky ways. Many
African societies sold condemned criminals into the slave trade,
which avoided the cost of prisons and brought the state some
revenue. Such prisoners also included the king's enemies and
other political opponents of the powerful, so that sale into the
trade served several ends. Some societies allowed a man to bring
judicial action against another man who committed adultery with
one of his wives. If convicted, the adulterer could be sold – to the
profit of the husband. One form of petty chicanery feeding the
slave trade was to use a young and attractive wife to entrap
victims.

Some West African societies made a distinction between two
kinds of warfare that are similar to the economic and political

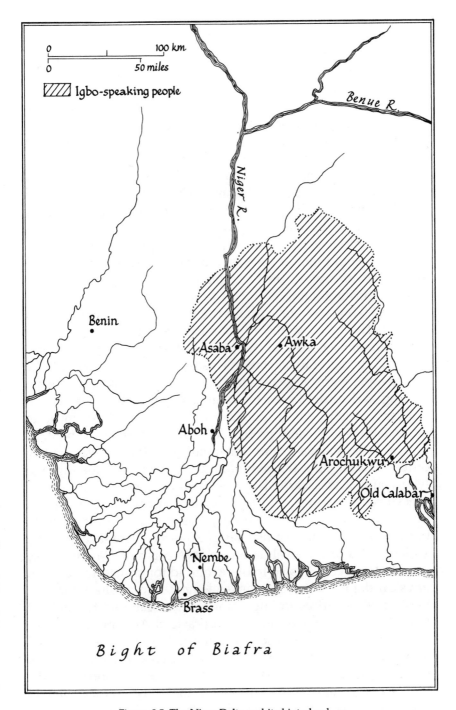

Figure 9.5 The Niger Delta and its hinterland.

models of enslavement. In the same Bambara region where the
kingdom of Segu emerged early in the eighteenth century,
tegereya, or banditry, is distinguished from *keleya*, or regular
warfare. *Tegereya* tended to emerge whenever the state's power to
keep the peace weakened. Young men from a single village or a
group of nearby villages got together on the pretext of going
hunting. Once away from home, they moved through the fallow
savanna country, mainly at night, until they were well away from
their own village. They then began stealing cattle and kidnapping
people, trying to pick up individuals or small groups, like women
on the way to the village well or others unlikely to be able to
defend themselves. The raiders were often a group of forty to fifty
men, who could fight if necessary, but they depended on stealth
and speed to capture their victims and sell them at a distance
before returning home.

Slave taking without warfare predominated in some African
regions. The Igbo country of southeastern Nigeria represents a
very different set of social and political circumstances from those
of Segu. The natural vegetation was high rain forest, though the
Ibgo people were densely settled there for centuries, practicing
shifting agriculture based on yams and palm oil. It was also a
stateless society, where public order was based on intricate
interrelations of kinship groups. The largest permanent political
unit was the village group, but political authority was widely
diffused throughout the community. Much of the trade through
Igbo country was carried by the Aro, an Igbo subgroup that
specialized in commerce. They had settlements widely scattered
throughout the region. Igbo society was not completely peaceful,
but compartively few of the slaves exported were taken in war.
Violence at a lower level, however, was common. Many people
were kidnapped and sold to the Aro; sold for crimes, for alleged
physical deformity, or after inveiglement into adultery; or contributed as sacrifices to important oracles scattered throughout
Ibo land – like the Aro's important oracle at Arochukwu. People
"sacrificed" to these oracles were not killed; they were spirited
away and sold into the slave trade. This Igbo pattern of
enslavement made it possible for the Igbo to respond to the
economic demand from buyers on the coast, rather than to
political events or natural disasters. As a result, the eighteenth-

century exports from the Bight of Biafra rose steadily, along with the steady rise in slave prices, rather than declining in spite of high prices (as in Senegambia) or rising far faster (as in Angola).

Rising demand – rising exports

During the course of the eighteenth century, slave prices in West Africa rose by a factor of three to four (Figure 9.2), and slave deliveries from most areas rose to match (Appendix Table 3 and Figure 9.3). In economic terms, the price elasticity of the supply of slaves appears to have been high; rising prices brought about rising deliveries. Unfortunately for historians, this kind of covariance cannot be taken as proof of cause and effect, but it did create a changing climate for economic decision making. An Asantehene, or king of Asante, no doubt assessed the pros and cons before engaging in a new war. He had to balance the advantages the Asante might win against the cost and risk. Somewhere in the equation was possible income from the sale of captives. The profit from sales of this kind were probably neither a necessary nor a sufficient cause to begin the war; but every rise in the price of slaves increased its weight in the equation, just as every rise in price increased the advantage of taking enemies captive rather than killing them.

But rising slave prices could increase the supply of slaves without necessarily encouraging warfare. When slave prices were low, merchants were limited in the distance they could profitably travel in search of captives. Rising prices meant that they could go farther afield. They could afford to spend more for guards, for food along the way, or for tolls and tariffs paid to states through which they passed. Such factors seem to account for the fact that in the course of the eighteenth century, slaves began to be drawn from places farther from the coast. Whereas most slaves in earlier centuries came from a zone within 50 or 100 miles from the coast, many by the early nineteenth century came from as far as 500 or even 1,000 miles away. This suggests that the political model of enslavement may still have been important – that high prices merely extended the reach of the trade.

Some of the high price elasticity in the supply of slaves also came from the response of the European slavers. As prices in the

Americas rose, they were able to offer higher prices on the African coast, but they were also well informed about conditions in Africa. They could therefore direct their ships to the places where supplies were increasing anyway in response to famine or anarchy – to the Congo region in the 1790s, for example.

Assessing the damage

An important debate has begun to emerge from recent research about the slave trade in Africa. It centers on the problem of assessing its damage to African societies. Defenders of the slave trade while it still existed argued that it was good for Africa, removing excess people, and good for the slaves themselves, bringing them into contact with Western civilization and the Christian religion. Such sentiments sound strange today, but the degree of damage to African societies is still an open question. A few historians would trace African "backwardness" to the influence of the slave trade, and some claim that most of Africa's present problems are traceable to the impact of the trade. Others concede that Africa was isolated from the main intercommunicating zones in world history, but they would otherwise deny the accusation of backwardness – an accusation drawn from Western cultural chauvinism and the old myths of African racial inferiority.

A satisfactory general assessment may never be possible, but some partial and tentative conclusions *are* possible. The most obvious is the fact that the slave trade affected different parts of Africa in different ways. Some small societies were completely destroyed; others were barely affected. Some simply refused to participate in the trade for long periods of time; the kingdom of Benin between the Igbo in the east and the Yoruba in the west, located on the "slave coast," is one example. Others societies devoted much of their common effort to exploiting the slave trade and turning it to their advantage at the expense of their neighbors.

From a high level of generalization, the slave trade appears as a stream of captives, leaving Africa in increasing numbers, with only an occasional decline, over a period of 200 years from the mid-seventeenth century to the mid-nineteenth. That picture is not inaccurate from the perspective of the whole Atlantic economy. Seen from the perspective of any region within Africa, however, the slave trade rarely lasted so long. Just as slave exports from the Senegambia peaked and then declined, those from other regions were rarely sustained from one decade to the next, perhaps because the human resources for export were no longer adequate. Even when high levels of exports from a particular coastal zone were sustained over long periods, as they were from West-Central Africa in the eighteenth century, the people for export came from many different and shifting sources in the interior. Slavery within Africa continued at some level throughout the whole period, but disastrous losses to a particular society from slave exports were rarely sustained for more than a few decades, leaving the possibility of recovery.

The destructiveness of the trade also varied with the form of enslavement. Where the economic model was predominant and led to wars carried out in order to capture slaves, the number of dead must have been several times the number captured and shipped to the coast or the Sahara. The middle-aged, the old, and the very young were often simply killed because their value to the trade was negligible. Politically inspired warfare was also enormously destructive, even though the slave trade was more a by-product than a cause.

Major catastrophes like the collapse of the Oyo Empire or the rise of new empires like the Caliphate of Sokoto in the early nineteenth century were especially destructive, but so were similar military and political movements after the mid-nineteenth century – when the Atlantic slave trade had effectively ended so far as West Africa was concerned.

At the other extreme, economically motivated enslavement through the judicial process, petty chicanery, exploitation of wives and adultery law, "sacrifice" to oracles, and even kidnapping involved comparatively little violence and loss of life. The enslaved were removed, which was certainly a loss in chronically underpopulated regions, but other damage was limited.

This is not to say that loss of life was negligible. Those who were enslaved as a result of famine died in enormous numbers before they could reach the coast. Others died of disease as they moved out of their home region into new disease environments. Even in the best circumstances, deaths in transit to the coast, in confinement awaiting shipment, and at sea on the way to the Americas must have taken 30 to 50 percent of those who began the journey. Most circumstances were less favorable.

Even so, and terrible as it was, if the slave trade is to be interpreted accurately, it has to be seen in the light of other human disasters. Warfare on other continents was also terrible. So was politically motivated destruction like the Nazi holocaust of the 1940s or the Stalinist destruction of the Soviet peasantry in the course of collectivization in the 1920s and 1930s. Climatic disasters like the most serious sahelian droughts probably killed an even higher proportion of the population over a considerable area, and they still take an enormous toll. So did the epidemiological disasters wrought by European diseases in the Americas in the sixteenth century and the Pacific islands in the nineteenth. The value in making these comparisons is not to apologize for the slave trade, but to help explain how West African societies managed to advance in so many areas of life during the era of the slave trade – and in spite of it.

Suggestions for further reading

Curtin, Philip D., *Economic Change in Pre-Colonial Africa: Senegambia in the Era of the Slave Trade* (Madison: University of Wisconsin Press, 1975).

Miller, Joseph C., *Way of Death: Merchant Capitalism and the Angola Slave Trade, 1730–1830* (Madison: University of Wisconsin Press, 1988).

Lovejoy, David E., *Transformations in Slavery: A History of Slavery in Africa* (Cambridge: Cambridge University Press, 1983).

Northrup, David, *Trade without Rulers: Pre-Colonial Economic Development in South-Eastern Nigeria* (Oxford: Clarendon Press, 1978).

10

Atlantic commerce in the eighteenth century

The tropical plantation had become, by the eighteenth century, a peculiarly specialized economic institution. It produced one or two products, which were sold at a great distance. The factors of production were not merely local land and capital, but capital and managerial labor from Europe, other workers from Africa, and associated products as diverse as Indian cloth to buy slaves, European cloth for them to wear, and New England barrel staves to make hogsheads for shipping sugar. The plantation complex, in short, was carried by oceanic trade over long routes stretching from the Pacific coast of Peru in the west to the Bay of Bengal in the east.

Bureaucrats and private traders

European intentions in the outer world had been clear from the earliest expeditions to India and the Antilles. Crown bureaucracies intended to make the overseas ventures profitable for the crown, producing either revenue for the monarch or power for the state – preferably both. Private traders had a lot in common with the free lances of the Spanish conquest. They were among the most self-interested and independent of the early capitalist firms. Though not always as violent and independent as the seventeenth-century buccaneers, they were equally anxious to evade control over their operations, and conditions were such that they were often successful.

European governments, even as late as the eighteenth century, had no way to reach or control individual enterprise. If they made general regulations, it was virtually impossible to enforce them.

The best they could do was to act through corporate groups like guilds. Some of these were natural corporations, like the group of people who practiced a particular craft in a particular place. The state could recognize such a group and give it legal existence as a guild, if it were not already organized in its own interest. If a natural group did not already exist, the state could create one, issuing a charter endowing a group of individuals with particular powers that had previously belonged to the crown. The basis was medieval concepts of law and government – as expressed in the feudalism from above of the earliest colonial efforts.

European governments had long used corporations of this kind to organize foreign trade, endowing guildlike corporations with the power to regulate the trade carried out by their members, but the profit or loss belonged to the individual member, not the guild. The Merchants of the Staple in the late medieval English wool trade was a regulatory corporation of this sort. Or the government might endow a corporation with power to carry out trade or production on the corporate account; these grants usually included the right to monopolize the trade of a particular area or in a particular commodity. Many of the early colonial corporations, like the Compagnie des îles d'Amérique, had the power to trade and operate plantations in their corporate capacity, but they were also endowed with some of the crown's legal jurisdiction. In cases of this kind, the crown did not need to enforce the monopoly. The self-interest of the corporation would see that it was enforced, if at all possible.

The greatest of the great colonial companies had been created in the seventeenth century to control trade and empire in eastern seas – usually defined as everything from the Cape of Good Hope to the western shores of the Americas. The Dutch East India Company, the English East India Company, and the French Compagnie des Indes are the prime examples that survived into the eighteenth century – operating their own armies and navies and fighting wars with each other as well as with the Asian powers. With such great power, these corporations became virtual branches of the European state, and the European governments found ways to influence their political moves while leaving their commercial monopolies untouched.

Commercial control in the Atlantic was rarely so neat, though each European power worked through a similar combination of institutional forms. Some powers organized proprietary colonies controlled by individuals or corporations – like Pennsylvania or Maryland or the early captaincies donatory of Brazil. Other colonies functioned under crown officials responsible directly to the government in Europe. Among these were the great bureaucratic structures like the great viceroyalties of New Spain and Peru, as well as smaller units like Jamaica, Barbados, or Saint Domingue in the Caribbean.

Companies had varied powers. The Dutch West India Company could govern as well as trade. The French Compagnie des Indes held various monopoly rights over the French slave trade, as well as its far greater rights in eastern seas. In the late seventeenth and early eighteenth centuries, the Royal African Company briefly held a monopoly over the English slave trade, but in the later eighteenth century the Company of Merchants Trading to Africa was only an infrastructural concern. All British merchants trading to Africa had to belong and support its activities, but these activities were limited to the control and management of forts and other trading posts on the African coast. In the third quarter of the eighteenth century, Portugal created commercial companies with limited monopoly rights over particular regions in Brazil, such as the Companhia Geral do Comércio de Pernambuco e Paraíba or the Companhia Geral do Comércio do Grão Pará e Maranhão. Even Spain, which used its imperial bureaucracy for most controls over the empire, sometimes granted company monopolies over the trade of particular ports.

At the center, each colonial power tended to have one or more agencies with general oversight of its overseas affairs. In Spain it was the Council of the Indies, and an equivalent body existed in Portugal. In France, it was the Ministère de la Marine – and so on, with other bodies like the Board of Trade and Plantations in Britain or the Casa de Contratación in Seville especially concerned with economic affairs.

Whatever the institutional forms, the European powers were agreed on the proper goal of commercial regulation: It was to make the state powerful and wealthy. The means were mercantilist economics, spelled out by publicists in the late seventeenth and early eighteenth centuries. One goal was a "favorable balance of trade," meaning an export balance with a consequent inflow of bullion. Colonial trade was to be carried by national shipping. The home country was to supply manufactured goods in return for raw materials. Ideally, each colonial power ruled over its national sector of the plantation complex and kept it hermetically sealed from contact with any other sector.

Such goals were impossible to achieve, as even the regulatory bodies came to recognize. Even without the additional problems of frequent wars throughout the eighteenth century, exceptions had to be allowed, and were allowed, from the beginning. Spain, having no African trading posts, allowed Portuguese and then other foreign shippers to supply slaves to the Spanish empire. The Dutch often operated as seaborne traders, with a minimal number of plantations under their own control. This meant that they worked to break into the sealed system of the others, rather than simutaneously trying to control one of their own. Even aside from legalized exceptions, thousands of individual shippers were willing and able simply to smuggle goods from one imperial system to another. To enforce a monopoly against such interlopers turned out to be impossible.

The reality of the eighteenth-century plantation trade is hard to discover in detail, simply because so much of it was extralegal. Some trade moved within the legal channels; much (probably most) of it did not. World trade in this period was also marked by broad flows of money and commodities. Silver from the Spanish Empire and gold from Brazil found their way into the hands of other Europeans – contrary to Spanish and Portuguese intentions. Those other Europeans, in turn, used monetary metals to finance their trade with the Indian Ocean – contrary to their own mercantilist and bullionist goals. In an unofficial and indirect way, then, bullion from the Americas paid for Europe's import from India.[1] A part of that larger transfer of goods and money passed through the plantation complex in ways far more intricate than some of the old stereotypes of the "triangular trade."

[1] Artur Attman, *American Bullion in the European Wold Trade 1600–1800* (Göteborg: Göteborgs Universitetsbibliotek, 1986).

Commodities in the African trade

Textbooks a few decades ago had a map showing African commerce in the era of the slave trade. The map showed a ship making its outward passage from Europe to West Africa with trinkets, arms, gunpowder, and gin to be exchanged for slaves. The ship carried the slaves to the West Indies in the middle passage and then picked up sugar, indigo, coffee, and other tropical products for the passage home. Ships did, in fact, make similar passages, but African commerce was far more complex.

For Africa the choice was not slave trade or no trade. Slaves were exported from western Africa over four centuries, but they were the most important single export for only a century and a half, from about 1690 to 1840. Certain regions sold slaves and little else over longer periods. West-Central Africa on either side of the Congo mouth was one. The so-called slave coast along the Bight of Benin (the present-day republic of Benin and western Nigeria) was another. Other regions sold slaves and other commodities as well. On the long coastline between the Gambia and the Gold Coast at the height of the slave trade, about three-quarters of all exports were in slaves; the rest were in pepper, ivory, and timber.

For other regions, about which we have more solid quantitative information, the picture was not very different. Senegambia, for example, was a heavy exporter of slaves in the early sixteenth century, following the breakup of the Jollof Empire. In the late sixteenth and early seventeenth centuries, however, its most important export to Europe was cowhides. Only in the 1680s did slaves again become more than 50 percent of Senegambian exports by value, fluctuating in the range of 60 to 90 percent of all exports through the 1780s. By the 1790s, gum Senegal, used in Europe for confectionery and printing, had replaced slaves as the main export. By the 1830s, the value of gum exports was already three times the value of slave exports at their peak; by the 1850s, the value of the gum trade was itself eclipsed by peanuts.

The Gold Coast (now Ghana) was another region with important trade other than slaves. From 1675 to 1731, the Dutch West India Company, which held a legal monopoly over Dutch trade in West Africa, carried far more gold than slaves. The annual average

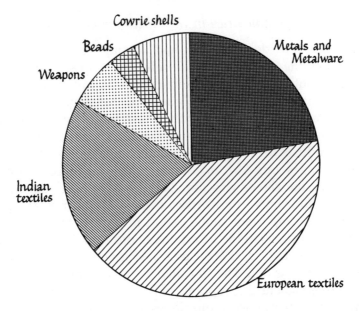

Figure 10.1 Royal Africa Company exports.

of these exports was 8,800 troy ounces, or 275 kilograms of pure metal – more than a quarter of a ton.

African trade, in short, was not solely for the support of the plantation complex, and these other currents of trade allowed African rulers to choose whether, or how much, they would be involved in the slave trade. On the import side, the anti-slave-trade publicists in Europe wanted to show that, in return for slaves, the Africans received nothing but trinkets of no real value – or else arms and liquor that were positively harmful. No one would be harmed, therefore, if the trade was abolished. In fact, the trinkets, liquor, and arms were far less important than the stereotype suggests, and other imports were more important.

Figures 10.1 and 10.2 illustrate the distribution of West African imports at two different periods, one in the late seventeenth century, as the slave trade began to escalate, and a second in the early nineteenth, when the slave trade had virtually ended for the Senegambia.[2] If they were drawn to scale, Figure 10.2 would be

---

[2] For Numerical equivalents see Appendix Table 3.

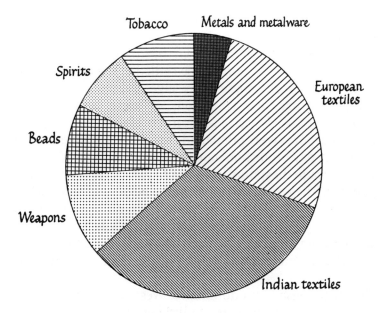

Figure 10.2 Imports to Senegambia.

vastly larger then Figure 10.1. Thus, the apparent decline in metal and metalware imports was not an actual decline; it was simply that, in the later period, metalware was a smaller proportion of a much larger total. Otherwise, the proportionate distribution of imports was not very different. Textiles made up more than half of the total in both periods, with an apparent gain of Indian over European textiles – a little surprising in a period when Europeans were beginning to produce cheap, machine-made cottons. Cowrie shells no longer figured as an important item, but liquor and tobacco now made up nearly a quarter of the total. This increase in luxury imports is largely accounted for by the fact that Africans now had more to spend abroad than they had had in the era of the slave trade. Even in this latter period, only about a third of the total imports fell into the "harmful" category.

The conduct of the African trade

The trade of the plantation complex crossed cultural boundaries at two points – on the Indian coast, where Europeans bought the

Indian textiles so important to the trade, and on the African coast itself. Over the very long run of history, the principal institution for cross-cultural trade had been the trade diaspora. Traders moving out from their home base settled at the important nodes of a trade network, made themselves familiar with the local language, culture, and conditions of trade, and then served traveling merchants as cross-cultural brokers.

Trade diasporas were often made up of peaceful merchants who preferred to pay protection money rather than fight. Not so for the European trade diasporas from the sixteenth century far into the eighteenth. They were armed from the beginning, and the period of no peace beyond the lines gave them still greater need for power to protect themselves from their fellow Europeans. The trade diasporas that operated on the African and Indian coasts were therefore militarized trade diasporas or trading post empires.

The Portuguese, who dominated West African trade until the mid-seventeenth century, made little effort to rule over African territory, basing their operations wherever possible on islands – the Cape Verde Islands off the Senegal coast, São Tomé off the Niger delta, and Luanda on the coast of Angola. This trade was regulated by the Casa da India in Lisbon, but it was not assigned to a single monopoly company. Cross-cultural brokerage was carried out by individual Portuguese or small Portuguese communities scattered along the coast and living under African political authorities.

In the middle third of the seventeenth century, other Europeans began to enter the trade. They quickly took up the alternative of chartered companies with monopoly rights and military as well as commercial authority from their home governments. These companies were especially common in the 1660s and 1670s – and on into the eighteenth century. They were expected to build and maintain expensive trade forts on the African coast to protect their onshore officials and their goods awaiting shipment. As relative peace returned, however, their position became untenable; European interlopers could trade freely on the African coast, and they had no permanent posts to maintain.

By the middle decades of the eighteenth century, interloper competition had destroyed the profits of the chartered companies so effectively that they were forced to change their function.

Instead of selling shipping services, they sold slaves to the interlopers. In effect, they used their shore establishments and their knowledge of local conditions to become middlemen and cross-cultural brokers, leaving the shipping business to others. Even this alternative was a stopgap. Interlopers could enter the brokerage business as easily as they had entered transatlantic shipping. Some of these shore-based interlopers were simply private Europeans who settled on the coast with African permission and began to accumulate slaves and other commodities for sale to European ships. Others were Africans who had learned European languages and enough about European ways to act as cross-cultural brokers on their own. They then began to handle the shoreside business of bulking cargo for shipment, leaving Europeans the shipping business alone. Given the disease cost of keeping European staff on the coast, this was a profitable division of labor for both sides.

The European powers were to return in greater strength in the nineteenth century, but in the eighteenth, Africans took over much of the brokerage function. On the Gambia it was especially important in the second half of the century. The Europeans still maintained some fortified posts, like the English trade castle on James Island in the mouth of the Gambia River, but the Africans were already managing most of the trade. When the French captured and destroyed the fort at James Island in 1779, the English did not bother to rebuild it, even after peace returned.

English and American ships still kept coming, and they fell into a pattern of trade relations determined by the African rulers and traders. The politics of trade at the Gambia mouth serve as an example. The kingdom of Niumi on the north shore of the river controlled all export trade, collecting tolls for anchoring or taking on wood and water. The chief port at the time was a set of four different trade enclaves located within a three-mile radius, each inhabited by a foreign merchant community. Each was allowed, for appropriate fees, to have extraterritorial jurisdiction over its own people, though all four were under the ultimate authority of the king of Niumi, represented locally by the *tubab mansa*, or commander of the foreigners. One of these enclaves was the French post at Albreda; a second was an Afro-Portuguese settlement at Siika. Malinke traders from the interior lived in

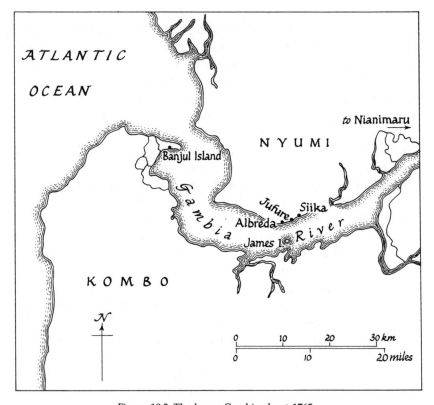

Figure 10.3 The lower Gambia about 1765.

Jufure, and the British had their own community and fort on James Island until 1779. The fact that the British island was fortified might suggest that it could lord it over a small state like Niumi, but that was not the case. The Gambia at that point is a tidal estuary, and James Island had no source of fresh water, which the garrison had to get from either shore, by permission from the African authorities.

All transactions in the river were subject to a regular *ad valorem* duty. If a ship sailed upriver to conduct trade in other kingdoms, Niumi authorities required it to take along brokers and translators, as well as an extra crew from Niumi. This helped to assure good behavior and to spare the European crew, but the crucial function was brokerage. A "chief linguister" went along in order to act as a broker for the ship's captain or supercargo. At an important point of trade like Nianimaru in the kingdom of Niani, the ship paid still more tolls.

That kingdom was also prepared to offer trade facilities to caravans from the interior. A caravan leader found himself in much the same position as the European ship's captain. He too had to turn to a local broker, in this case a *jaatigi*, or landlord-broker, who could offer lodging for the caravan's personnel, including slaves in transit. The actual bargain was struck by the chief linguister and the *jaatigi*, each acting on behalf of his own principal, in return for appropriate fees. Thus, the foreign Africans and overseas traders both found that they could do business without necessarily knowing the local language, and the local people shared in their profits.

Merchants and planters

Once at sea, Atlantic commerce followed the norms of Western commercial culture, though a common culture was no guarantee of trade without conflict. Commercial rivalry played a large role in European international rivalry, and groups of people with different roles in the plantation complex were rivals of a different sort. The most common friction was between merchants and planters, and it took different forms in different national segments of the plantation complex.

In the French segment, the planter grew the cane, manufactured the raw sugar, and carried it to the dock. There his responsibility ended. He sold his product to a local merchant or a local agent of a French commercial house, who took over the responsibility of transporting it to France for sale. The merchant thus acquired the right to any residual profits that might occur. Negotiations between planter and merchant were therefore crucial, because they determined the way the final sale price would be divided between the production and service sectors – that is, between planters and merchants-shippers. Planters found these negotiations unsatisfactory, partly because the colonies had few sources of credit. For lack of banking facilities, planters were at the mercy of local merchants and ships' masters who happened to be in port. Many transactions between French planters and merchants were a disguised form of barter. If a French vessel turned up with a cargo of slaves, they were sold for a price expressed in *livres tournois* (the French currency of the time). The captain or supercargo then bargained separately over the price of sugar, indigo, or cotton, also expressed in *livres*. But no physical *livres* were present; they were simply a currency of account, and goods were exchanged for goods, balanced by credit extended by the merchant to the planter for any shortfall. Planters found themselves chronically in debt, and the debt increased gradually with time. The planter was thus tied to his creditor firm, with its home office in Nantes or some other Atlantic port, and his freedom of action was further reduced.

By the 1780s, the web of credit was an acute source of tension between the planters and their French business contacts, and between the planters and the home country as a whole. Planters suspected that the merchants and their friends had influence at court and could manipulate the whole colonial–metropolitan relationship in their own interest. Planters had the theoretical advantage of a protected metropolitan market for their product, but French-produced sugar was cheapest and most competitive in other markets. They gained nothing from tariff protection. They also knew that the things they had to buy – slaves and provisions – were cheaper from non-French sources. The North Americans had the cheapest provisions; British slavers, the cheapest slaves. French planters did, in fact, buy provisions for the North Americans and Dutch and slaves from the English, but the web of credit binding them to particular French firms made smuggling more difficult than it might have been otherwise. Like the British North Americans of the 1760s and 1770s, they saw the colonial system of trade controls as one imposed from France and serving French interests.

British trade was organized differently, and the economic position of Jamaica was a little different from that of Saint Domingue. Planters had legal access to North American and Irish provisions, and British sugar duties protected Jamaican sugar in the British market. From about 1740 on, English sugar prices were higher than those elsewhere, which meant that British trade controls worked in favor of the British West Indian planters.

Planter resentment of the home country was also moderated by the usual relationship between planters and merchants. Instead of selling in the colony, the British planter shipped his crop to Europe on his own account, where a merchant firm sold it on commission. The planter, not the merchant, was therefore the residual claimant on the final value of the product.

The British sugar merchant also performed a variety of other services. When he sold the crop, he held the balance for the planter, and the planter could therefore draw bills on the merchant for a variety of expenses. If a planter needed slaves, he could pay with a bill drawn on the merchant house. If he need supplies or stores from Britain, he could write to his English agent with a shopping list – again paid for out of sale receipts, with another commission to the merchant house.

It goes without saying that this relationship also involved credit. It was all too easy for the planter to overdraw his account, but that suited both parties well enough. The planter could live like a gentleman, either in England or in the colony. The merchant was glad to lend money on the good security of a sugar estate. The merchants' chief source of profit, indeed, was the interest on these loans. The prevalence of absenteeism among the British planting class meant that both merchants and proprietors of estates were often resident in Britain, so that whatever tensions between them did exist were not automatically translated into friction between colony and metropolis. But the very fact that the colonial trade system tended to favor the planters meant that New England traders and others found cause to evade the law.

Caribbean trade

Trade flowed in a variety of channels, often outside the idealized national monopolies, and even outside the legal exceptions colonial powers had been forced to allow. Instead of the over-simplified triangular trade, a variety of multilateral trading voyages was possible. A New England ship might sail to Jamaica with a cargo of barrel staves, horses, and salt fish. These could be sold for bullion, derived in turn from smuggling slaves into Spanish America – and Jamaica was the main entrepôt for that trade. In addition, the captain might buy a few slaves for sale on the North American mainland, but his "middle passage" would carry him only to Saint Domingue to complete his cargo with sugar and molasses, bought with bullion. On the way north, he could stop in Chesapeake Bay to sell the slaves, then back to New England, where he would sell the molasses to be made into rum for the fur trade. The French sugar could then be relabeled "product of the British West Indies" for sale in Britain, where it and any leftover bullion could pay for British manufactures wanted in New England.

Or a French ship might make the outward voyage to Africa, pick up a cargo of slaves, but sell it in Spanish America for bullion. The bullion, in turn, found its way to the Compagnie des Indes for shipment to southern India in return for indigo-died cloths of a kind much in demand in Senegal. These cloths might be sold in Senegal – not for slaves, but for gum and for Senegalese cloths in demand farther down the coast in Dahomey. The Dahomean slaves would be sold, in turn, in the New World, and variants of the same cycle could be played out again.

The exchanges that might be profitable an any moment changed constantly with markets, prices, war and peace, and a whole range of other conditions. It is, however, possible to make some broad generalizations about the flow of Caribbean trade in reality – as opposed to theory. Some trade did actually flow in legal channels as it was supposed to do, within a single imperial system. Much of it flowed outside those channels. The Dutch and Danes, with only a small plantation complex of their own, systematically supplied other people's colonies with slaves and took off tropical products out of the proceeds. English slave dealers supplied their own colonies and a good deal more. As a result, they built up balances in foreign colonies that could be used to buy bullion from Spanish America, sugar and molasses from the French islands, and a variety of other products. French sugar supplied the French market and good deal more. Finally, everyone, including a few Spanish shippers, carried the trade of Spanish America.

To maintain this degree of separation between theory and reality imposed certain strains on European governments, strains eased in some cases by liberal bribery and tolerated in others with a pretense of ignorance justified as "benign neglect." As time passed, however, some of the strains became more serious. When the time of crisis came, they were exposed and took their place alongside other tensions that ushered in the age of democratic revolution.

Suggestions for further reading

Curtin, Philip D., *Cross-Cultural Trade in World History* (New York: Cambridge University Press, 1984).

Chaudhuri, K.N., *Trade and Civilisation in the Indian Ocean: An Economic History from the Rise of Islam to 1750* (Cambridge: Cambridge University Press, 1985).

Clark, John G., *La Rochelle and the Atlantic Economy During the Eighteenth Century* (Baltimore: John Hopkins University Press, 1981).

Pares, Richard, *A West India Fortune* (London: Longmans, 1950).

Sheridan, Richard, *Sugar and Slavery: An Economic History of the British West Indies, 1623–1775* (Aylesbury: Ginn, 1974).

Solow, Barbara L., and Stanley L. Engerman (eds.), *Caribbean Slavery and British Capitalism* (New York: Cambridge University Press, 1988). See also Vol. 17, No. 4, of the *Journal of Interdisciplinary History*, Spring 1987.

Viliers, Patrick, *Traite des noirs et navires négrier au XVIIIe siècle* (Grenoble: Éditions des 4 seigneurs, 1982).

The Democratic Revolution in the Atlantic basin

1700's

The institutions of the plantation complex reached their apogee in the third quarter of the eighteenth century. They then began to come apart for reasons that were partly internal, arising from the workings of the system itself, and partly external, from events in the greater world of European influence in the Atlantic basin. Some seeds of its destruction had been present as contradictions within the plantation complex from the beginning; others only emerged in the nineteenth century. In any event, the social and economic patterns that had governed the plantation world of the American tropics began to be dismantled during a "long century" lasting from about 1770 to 1890.

The Democratic Revolution

The fall of the plantation complex was associated with a broader set of political changes that sometimes go by the name of the "Democratic Revolution" – a phrase that groups together a series of political revolutions around the Atlantic rim. The first was the American Revolution of 1776–83, but Spanish and Portuguese attempts at imperial reform in the 1760s and 1770s were at least precursors. The American Revolution not only helped to formulate the ideology of the democratic revolutions that followed; it also brought, in time, the end of slavery in the northern United States. The French Revolution followed in 1789 – partly sparked by the American. The high cost of French participation in the American War for Independence was an important reason why

144

the French government was forced to call a meeting of the Estates General in 1789. The French Revolution, in turn, swept away the institutions of the Old Regime in most of Western Europe. The Napoleonic Wars that followed included the capture of Spain and the effective, if temporary, decapitation of the Spanish Empire in 1808, which opened the way for further revolts on the inititative of the Spanish American colonies. Even Britain passed through its own crisis of limited democratization with the passage of Reform in 1832. The Reform Act, in turn, made possible the passage of the Emancipation Act for the British Empire in 1833. France freed the colonial slaves as a by-product of its Revolution of 1848. Finally, emancipation came to Cuba and Brazil in the 1880s in a political process intertwined with an independence movement in Cuba and the end of the Brazilian Empire.

Industrialism, capitalism, and imperialism

To understand these revolutions in comparative context, it is important to move to higher realms of generalization. The events of the broad Democratic Revolution were partly founded on a more fundamental change in human affairs. It is sometimes called the "Industrial Revolution" and seen as a partner or twin of the much earlier Agricultural Revolution beginning in about 10,000 B.C.

Perhaps the term "revolution" is a misnomer, since it suggests a period of rapid change followed by a new period of comparative stability. What happened in both cases was somewhat different. A new level of technological expertise made it possible for human beings to organize their societies in ways that were absolutely new. Before the Agricultural Revolution, most people gained their livelihood from hunting, fishing, or gathering. Most lived in small bands with frequent movement. After the coming of agriculture, populations could become denser. Cities and literacy came into existence, and the pace of change in human societies became much more rapid than it had been in the past.

Then, many centuries later, a second change of similar magnitude began. Before the eighteenth century, most people in most societies were tied to food production. The standard of living for ordinary people was so low that life was a constant struggle for survival. The nineteenth century was the crucial period of transition. By the early twentieth, many societies had moved to a new state of affairs, in which food production could be left to a small minority, and levels of production and consumption for the great majority were higher than at any other time in history. The pace of change in technology became more rapid than it had ever been in the past, and the pace of change in all aspects of human society seemed to accelerate. The coming of industrial technology therefore took on the appearance of a permanent revolution.

The very existence of such fundamental changes raises some problems of high-level generalization about cause and effect, dependent and independent variables. In very broad terms, historians and others talk about three phenomena that came to be interrelated in important ways in the later eighteenth century and on into the nineteenth – and have remained interrelated up to the present.

These phenomena are industrialism, capitalism, and imperialism. "Industrialism," in this broad sense, is taken to mean the whole of industrial technology. "Capitalism" is a way of organizing the production of goods and services whereby control over the process and the product rests with those who made the capital investment. "Imperialism" is the process by which Western states and some others created territorial empires in the non-Western world.

Some authorities see capitalism as the independent variable and the other two as its consequences. Others claim that the Industrial Revolution was itself built on the profits of earlier adventures overseas. Still others find that industrial technology and the flow of goods it created made possible both modern capitalist institutions and the European conquest of much of the rest of the world in the nineteenth century. A satisfactory balance among these conflicting claims may not be possible, but it is clear that these three phenomena were related in complex ways over the past two centuries. Their relationships changed through time, and the phenomena themselves changed through time. Capitalism in 1830 was not the capitalism of 1930 or of 1980; nor was the industrial technology of 1890 the same as that of 1990.

From that analytical stratosphere, it may be well to drop to a lower level to consider the Democratic Revolution in Europe and

America between about 1780 to 1830. The term revolution is itself a problem. It has many meanings. The American Revolution was obviously not a revolution in the same sense that the Industrial Revolution was. (And you can always find someone to argue that neither was a revolution of any kind.) It seems clear, however, that Western countries in the modern period sometimes pass through periods when social and political change is more rapid than usual, when control over the institutions of the state and society passes to new groups of people.

The Democratic Revolution of the late eighteenth and early nineteenth centuries was a series of revolutions in that sense. Most historians deal with the prerevolutionary period as the Old Regime, a period of comparatively slow political change, when Europeans had reached a series of compromises in intellectual, political, and social life. The democratic revolutions broke this equilibrium of the Old Regime in Europe, and the classic case is the French Revolution. But the equilibrium of the Old Regime also extended to the whole of the Atlantic world. It was broken there as well in ways that are not usually associated with the better-known democratic revolutions in France or North America.

Background: Economic, social, and political.

The European background is important. On the economic side, the Democratic Revolution ran parallel in time to the first phase of the Industrial Revolution – whatever the cause-and-effect relationship. In the background of both were intellectual patterns like the seventeenth-century rise of natural science leading to the Newtonian synthesis. Another background factor was better communication, with roads, canals, and tramways speeding up economic life and exchange. The cost of ocean shipping had decreased systematically since the sixteenth century, and that decrease continued throughout the eighteenth. It was one of the important conditions that made the intricate trade network of the plantation complex possible. Better agricultural technology also helped to raise European living standards in the eighteenth century.

Earlier contact with the overseas world had an influence as well. Some have claimed that the profits of the plantation complex helped to finance a major part of British industry. Most historians now disagree, but it is clear that one important input from the new World was not profits but technology. The Europeans had transferred American crops – maize, manioc, potatoes, cacao, peanuts, pineapples, and many more – to other parts of the world, including Europe. Potatoes became a major source of food in Europe by the eighteenth century. Maize was on its way to becoming a major source of cattle feed, hence providing an indirect increase of protein in European diets. The new crops helped to make possible a population increase in Europe, as they did in China and throughout the tropical world.

The European population increase came from other sources as well. From the middle of the eighteenth century on, Europe passed through a mortality revolution. That revolution was once associated with the achievements of scientific medicine, but the real achievements of modern medicine hardly go back before the early applications of the germ theory of disease in the 1880s and 1890s, and the mortality revolution came much earlier. The earliest phases of this revolution are now associated with improvements in general cleanliness beginning in the eighteenth century and continuing with improved water supplies and sewage systems even before people realized that they were reducing the germs and insects to carry them – as well as removing refuse and offensive smells.[1]

Preindustrial societies were generally characterized by high birth rates and high death rates. Postindustrial societies can maintain their numbers with far fewer births, because their death rates are so much lower. At the first stage, the declining death rate of the mortality revolution produced population growth – which could be supported by the crops and the new food technology. At a later stage, fertility in the West declined as well, and the explosive growth of population leveled off. Meanwhile, the population explosion that began about 1750 provided the added people to work the new machines and to move to the overseas settlement areas in the nineteenth century.

[1] James C. Riley, *The Eighteenth-Century Campaign to Avoid Disease* (London: Macmillan, 1987); Philip D. Curtin, *Death by Migration* (New York: Cambridge University Press, 1989).

Economic growth in the late preindustrial period brought social change as well. The new wealth was not distributed in the same way as the older wealth. Merchants and certain landed groups profited more than the old nobility, whose incomes remained relatively unchanged. All of these people were members of a tightly stratified society where rank and status were set. For some of the newly rich, they were set at relatively low levels. New wealth no longer conformed to old rank. This fact led to resentment on both sides.

On the political side, the governments of the Old Regime had little freedom of movement in spite of the fact that power was more centralized than it had been a century or so earlier. Monarchs rarely reached their subjects directly. At home, as in their dealings with maritime traders, they ruled through and with the consent of a web of legal cooperations from the level of craft guilds and merchant guilds through the universities to corporate entities like the Estates of the realm or the church. This meant that governments could not easily adjust social and political status and privilege to fit the facts of changing wealth – especially new wealth in the hands of such groups as the newly rich bourgeoisie. It might even be said that the essential compromise of the Old Regime was to maintain ancient privilege while adding new privilege as a way of keeping the whole structure from foundering.

The Enlightenment

Intellectual changes in Europe had implications for the overseas world, as well as for Europe itself. The Enlightenment – the eighteenth-century interest in applying reason to human affairs – was crucial. Publicists of the Enlightenment, sometime called *philosophes*, were fond of pointing out irrational elements in economic, social, or political organization. They were concerned about privilege without equivalent functions in society, and they sometimes demanded legal equality before the law for all subjects.

They were not necessarily partisans of representative government, much less democrats in any recent sense of the term. Many, if not most, were more interested in rationality and efficiency in government. If this could be imposed from above, so much the better; hence their call for "enlightened despotism." To this end, the enlightened publicists could work with and through monarchs who were also interested in increasing royal power at the expense of the church, the nobility, and corporate bodies of all kinds. The attachment of rationality to the effort was new, but the main directions were not very different from the goals of monarchs and crown advisors since the days of Ferdinand and Isabella. Whether the *philosophes* sought to work through the monarchs or not, they were enemies of ancient privilege, and ancient privilege was thoroughly built into the political and social structures.

One aspect of special importance for the plantation complex was the attack on slavery. The early-eighteenth-century rights-of-man philosophy was accepted by many of the enlightened, but it had to do with the rights of the eighteenth-century bourgeoisie, not those of colonial slaves. Slave emancipation for the colonies was an insignificant item on the agenda of European reformers until after the French Revolution had begun.

But the Enlightenment contained and popularized a kind of exoticism and a particular view of the non-Western world. Europeans in the sixteenth and seventeenth centuries had been fascinated by the outer world. Rousseau's idea that man was not naturally corrupt, but had been corrupted by society, entered in the eighteenth. Savages, having no civilized society, might be taken to be "natural men" and thus "uncorrupted men" or even "good men." This was, perhaps, more a part of the romantic movement than of the Enlightenment in its earlier phases, but it led Europeans to weaken some of their natural xenophobia. They became more interested in and sympathetic to people of differing cultures. This came in time to include colonial slaves, and it thus helped to bring them within the realm in which the rights of man might be thought to operate.

Finally, popular piety – more a reaction to the rationalism of the Enlightenment than a part of it – began to be important in the late eighteenth century, especially in England. It was a short step from the new fervor of Christian belief to a new level of Christian action. Christian action called for the eradication of evil; colonial slavery and the slave trade seemed to be one of the most striking evils. It was one of the first targets of Christain reformers. These reformers, however, came into a share of power *after* the democratic revolutions were successful in Europe, not before. It was only in the 1780s, at the earliest, that colonial slaves began to find a place within the rights-of-man philosophy – at least a half-century lag behind similar demands for Europeans.

Reform of the overseas colonies meant something quite different to the supporters of enlightened despotism. It had overtones of the old battles between bureaucrats and free lances, and now the bureaucrats wanted once more to establish their own control over the colonies in the name of enlightened rationality. Sometimes they succeeded and sometimes they failed. They succeeded in the case of the Spanish Bourbons, who actually did reform the administration of the Spanish Empire and liberalize the commercial system from the 1770s on. Similar reforms in Portuguese America succeeded to a lesser degree under the "Marquês de Pombal" as Minister of the Navy and the Overseas Territories in the 1750s and 1760s. The British succeeded in reforming the British East India Company and bringing it under the control of the crown, but they failed after 1763 in their efforts to make the British North American colonies pay part of the cost of their own defense. The French and Dutch made fewer efforts; their colonies entered the era of the democratic revolutions even more in need of reform. As a result, the political structure of the overseas colonies remained frozen in something like the balance of the political compromise that emerged toward the end of the seventeenth century.

Realignments in the colonial world

While Europe itself was outgrowing the compromises of the Old Regime, the world of Europeans overseas was doing the same, though in different spheres and in differing ways. One of the major changes overseas in the eighteenth century was a shift in the forms of European colonial activity. In the sixteenth century, the Portuguese had begun with a trading post empire in eastern seas, later imitated by others, like the Dutch and English East India companies. The Spanish conquest of Mexico and Peru had opened a sphere of territorial empire in the New World. After the 1550s, the Portuguese transferred the plantation complex to Brazil, whence it had spread successively to the north and west.

These three spheres – trading post, territorial empire, and

plantation complex – continued and even grew in the eighteenth
century, but significant changes took place as well. The English
and Dutch East India companies began to convert their trading
post operations into territorial empire, with government responsibility over alien populations. By the end of the century, the English
East India Company had become the most important ruling
power on the Indian subcontinent, and the Dutch East India
Company was the effective ruler of Java. The plantation complex
was still highly valued in Europe, but in the nineteenth century
India would mean more to Britain than the West Indies did, and
Java would mean more to the Netherlands than Surinam and
Curaçao did.

At the same time, the population explosion in Europe implied
a population explosion among the European settlers overseas, and
larger numbers of Europeans than ever moved overseas to
settlement regions like the United States. Settlement colony
populations grew rapidly from internal population growth as
much as from immigration. Spanish America had turned from a
true empire into a plural society – largely through the natural
increase of the white population, alongside no increase or slow
increase among the Indians. Much the same happened to the
French in Quebec and the Dutch at the Cape of Good Hope. These
were intended as trade enclaves, not true colonies, but population
growth had made them that. Europeans overseas in all three
sectors – empire, settlement, plantation – were coming to believe
that their interests and those of the metropolis were very different.

This unintended shift from trading post to territorial empire,
from territorial empire to plural society, and from small colony to
big colony had a number of consequences. Among the most
important was a need to readjust the political and economic
structures of empire. New interests and demands had emerged
within a political structure based on something quite different. In
England, for example, a new East India interest rose in Parliament
to confront the established West India interest. In the British
Empire overseas, British North America grew too big for its old
place in the plantation complex. It produced more supplies than
the British West Indies could consume. These supplies were
therefore sold to the French West Indies as well, but the sales were
illegal and opposed by the mother country. The result was to set

North Americans and French West Indian planters in opposition to the trade laws binding their respective empires.

Similar differential growth took place in Spanish America. Venezuela, Colombia, Chile, and Argentina all grew economically in the eighteenth century much more rapidly than Peru or New Spain did. These growing colonies also produced hides, coffee, tobacco, and other products that Spain could not consume. But an industrializing Britain stood ready to buy them and to sell cheap manufactures in return. To the degree that the Spanish government tried to prevent a shift in trade away from metropolitan Spain, it alienated these colonies.

New colonial wealth overseas, in short, was not distributed geographically in the same way it had previously been. This differential growth was similar to the new distribution of wealth between the social classes in Europe and in the North American colonies. Just as new wealth set up tensions between social classes within Europe and North America, it set up tensions between geographical units in several of the far-flung empires. These strained relations between the frontier regions of European empire and the metropolis at home were to become an important theme in the process and outcome of several of the democratic revolutions.

Democratic revolutions and the plantation complex

In the transatlantic world under European control, each new phase of the democratic revolutions sent out shock waves to other parts of the broader Atlantic world. Each revolution was, first of all, an example that others might copy. Even more, each revolutionary change anywhere in an interrelated Atlantic world tended to create further maladjustments in other regions. The American Revolution, for example, was a revolt of the frontier against the metropolis. It was also partly a social revolution and a political revolution establishing a new order within the thirteen colonies. Aside from its exemplary role, it influenced other parts of the plantation complex in several different ways. It decreased the prosperity of the British West Indies by breaking the traditional tie to the mainland colonies as a source of cheap provisions. It brought about the first emancipation of slaves, and news of emancipation in the northern colonies passed quickly into the tropical Atlantic. This news may not have reached or influenced the mass of Caribbean slaves, but it did reach their masters, who were chronically nervous about slave revolts anyway.

In France, the American Revolution not only helped to bankrupt the government, it also served as an example of a "good" revolution, one that seemed to do away with aristocratic priviledge, bring the middle class to power, and yet not cause the working class to become too uppity or demanding of further extensions of liberty.

In the French West Indies, the lesson was read in another way. The planting class saw the American revolt principally as a rebellion against the "colonial compact" of tightly controlled trade with the mother country under the mercantilist prescriptions. It was a rebellion of the political periphery against the core, and one that worked without seeming to disrupt other relations in society. It had been carried out without a serious slave revolt in the South, even though the British had occasionally promised freedom in order to recruit slaves belonging to rebel masters. (At least one of George Washington's slaves from Mount Vernon responded to that call.) From the French West Indies, though, the American Revolution looked like a safe revolution.

The trail of consequences from the French Revolution was far more complex. Overseas, it fundamentally unsettled the whole social, political, and economic order that had constituted the plantation complex at it peak. First, it led directly to a series of revolts in the colony of Saint Domingue, initially by the planting class, then by the colored class, the *gens de couleur*, and finally by the slaves themselves. By 1804, Haiti had become an independent republic, and the most important single sugar colony had dropped from the complex. The revolution in France also brought on revolutions in Guadeloupe and Martinque, though with different aims and less success.

And it had ramifications elsewhere in the Caribbean. Fear of a similar slave revolt was especially strong in Jamaica, and British troops from Jamaica intervened in the revolutionary wars on Saint Domingue. After the French planters lost in Saint Domingue, many fled to Jamaica. The general uncertainty of the mid-1790s was one cause of a Maroon War, though the war itself was more nearly European aggression against the maroons that a maroon threat to the planting order – and the maroons lost. More important still, the disappearance of Saint Domingue sugar from world markets opened the way to one more stage in the sugar migration that had begun in the eastern Mediterranean. This step carried it to Cuba and Puerto Rico, which began to import slaves in the 1790s and shortly began their own sugar revolution in the early nineteenth century.

Counterrevolution in Spanish America

The third episode of revolution was the series of revolts and civil wars in Spanish America. They tend to be lumped together as the Spanish-American "wars for independence" and are sometimes equated with the North American war for independence. But this puts them in the wrong perspective. The outcome may have been independence from Spain, but these revolts were very different from the French or American revolutions, and each was different from the others.

One reason they tend to be superfically the same is a matter of timing. They all began about 1809, and the results were in by about 1825. This, however, was a function of Spanish political history. The reforms of the 1770s had been enough to hold off the danger of rebellion for the time being, and Spain had been strong enough to suppress further demands during the earlier phases of the general Democratic Revolution. For that matter, most of Spanish America was a plural society, with a large population of Indians, mestizos, and Afro-American slaves. These non-Spanish groups, sometimes called *castas*, lacked the power to revolt successfully on their own, and the upper classes could not revolt against Spain without endangering their own position at home.

In 1808, however, Napoleon captured Spain and effectively cut off the Spanish Empire overseas. Each colony was now on its own. This situation opened the way to the full and untrammeled influence of every suppressed rivalry, resentment, or unsatisfied ambition previously stifled by Spanish rule. In some places, the situation disintegrated into a struggle for power between important local familes and the Spanish officials left out on a limb by the disppearance of a Spanish government they could recognize. In other places, men who were moved by the ideals of the Democratic Revolution tried to put themselves at the head of political movements to achieve the rights of man in their own countries – men like Simón Bolívar in some moods, Father Morelos of Mexico, and perhaps Bernardo O'Higgins of Chile.

In still other places, men with military command simply took over because they, and they alone, had the power to take political control. As a group, these men were called caudillos. They sometimes represented the social goals and interest of the creole, or non-Spanish-born ruling class, or they might represent little more than their own desire for power or wealth. Among the men in this class were António Lopez de Santa Anna in Mexico or Juan Manuel de Rosas in Argentina.

Although these revolts and coups d'etat and wars involved independence from Spain, independence was rarely the fundamental issue. It could jump from the left to the right of the political spectrum with changes in Spanish politics. When Spain developed the liberal consitution of 1812, American opponents of the Democratic revolution opposed union with Spain. When Spain was safely conservative, the local ruling class favored Spanish rule, and partisans of the Democratic Revolution opposed it.

Whatever the twists and turns of the Spanish American wars of independence, the Democratic Revolution lost out. This was true as well in Brazil, where local aristocrats managed to break away peacefully from Portugal in the early 1820s. It was also true in Cuba, where the ultimate victory of the Spanish Conservatives preserved Cuba from the corrosive influence of the rights of man, and the slave regime was able to continue into the 1880s. Although some independent republics emancipated their slaves in the first half of the nineteenth century, the failure of the Democratic Revolution in Cuba and Brazil was part of the background that allowed the plantation complex there to go on to new triumphs in the nineteenth century.

Suggestion for further reading

Bethell, Leslie (ed.), *The Cambridge History of Latin America*, Vol. 2 (Cambridge: Cambridge University Press, 1984).

Davis, David Bryan, *The Problem of Slavery in the Age of Revolution, 1770–1812* (Ithaca: Cornell University Press, 1975).
Slavery and Human Progress (London: Oxford University Press, 1984).
Palmer, Robert R., *The Age of Democratic Revolution*, 2 vols. (Princeton: Princeton University Press, 1959–64).

12

Revolution in the French Antilles

The slave rebellion that began in 1791 and led to the independence of Haiti in 1804 was the key revolution in the fall of the plantation complex. It not only ended the slave regime on the French half of the island; it also made Haiti the first European colony with a non-European population to achieve independence and formal, if somewhat grudging, recognition as a member of the community of Western nations.

The Haitian revolution was also the most violent step toward the end of the plantation complex. Its only rival in violence was the American Civil War some seventy years later; but North American plantations were marginal to the complex, and the American Civil War was fought about other issues as well as slavery. The French Antilles, on the other hand, were central to the slave regime in the Caribbean, and the Caribbean was central to the whole plantation complex in the late eighteenth century.

Geography of the French Antilles

The large colony of Saint Domingue was the heart of the French Caribbean as of the 1780s, even more so than Jamaica was in the British Caribbean. But Saint Domingue was not a single social and economic unit in the same way Jamaica was. It was divided into three separate provinces that communicated with France and with one another by sea. Each province was socially and economically distinct; each was focused on its own urban center or centers. The provinces were just as much separate entitites as were the two

158

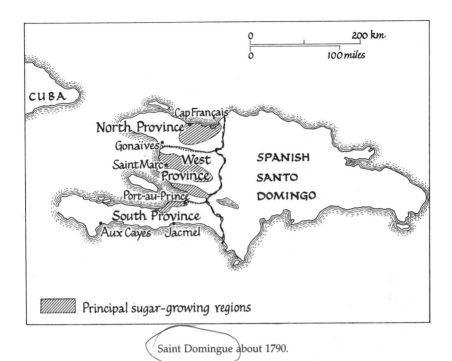

Saint Domingue about 1790.

islands colonies of Guadeloupe and Martinique. In that sense, the French Caribbean consisted of five island colonial units, plus Cayenne, or French Guiana.

The geography of Saint Domingue was largely responsible for the division of the colony into three separate units. The western end of the islands is shaped like a U with its top to the west – the two arms of the U being long peninsulas formed by mountain ranges that take off from the central massif along the French–Spanish border. The colony could therefore be approached from the north coast, the south coast, or the central bay.

The North Province included the northern peninsula stretching to the west, but it centered on the lowlands of the north coast. The *plaine du nord* was the best sugar land on the island, with the largest concentration of estates and the most valuable estates. Cap Français was its metropolis, the largest town in the whole colony, and the capital.

The West Province was not west at all, but central. Unlike the north, it was split topographically into three areas of good sugar land, each with its own small town centers. These were the Valley of the Artibonite, shipping through the ports of Saint Marc and Gonaïves; the valley of the cul-de-sac, shipping through Port-au-Prince, capital of the province; and the coastal plain around Léogane.

The South Province was mainly the southern peninsula stretching to the west, rugged and mountainous, with only pockets of good sugar land along the coasts. Its main product was coffee, grown in the mountains on many comparatively small estates. With smaller estates, the proprietors were less wealthy than the sugar planters of the coastal plains; more of the proprietors were men of color; and the provincial society was less tightly stratified, though a tense rivalry existed between the colored and white castes. The only urban centers were small and scattered port towns – Jérémie, Aux Cayes, and Jacmel.

Below the provincial level was the parish – as in Jamaica or Louisiana – equivalent to a North American county. The parishes were the basic units of local government and militia organization, and the first rung for the formation of planter opinion or political action of any kind.

Martinique and Guadeloupe were again different. Each centered on a single important volcanic island rising from the sea. The good sugar land was found on the skirt of the mountain, on alluvial soil created by erosion from the volcano itself. Guadeloupe as a political unit included some minor islands along with Basse Terre, with its volcano and sugar land. Grande Terre just alongside lacked the altitude necessary to tap the moisture of the northeast trade winds. Martinique and Guadeloupe were each about the size of one of Saint Domingue's provinces, and the patterns of colonial life in each were as distinctive as they were in the provinces of Saint Domingue.

Social structure and social tensions

The social structure of Saint Domingue was much like that of other West Indian colonies of the period; but class and caste divisions were more aggravated here than elsewhere, and the conflict with the metropolis was more serious. In caste terms, the numerical breakdown in the late 1780s was 40,000 whites, 28,000 free colored, and 452,000 slaves – 8, 5, and 87 percent, respectively. Caste relations had been deteriorating in the 1770s and 1780s. Growing demand for Saint Domingue sugar had increased slave imports, whereas the white population had been stable for several decades. The planters drove the slaves harder to meet the increased demand for their products. Saint Domingue had more proprietors and wealthy whites in residence than was common on most British Caribbean islands. Resident owners used slaves as domestics, which increased the proportion of house to field slaves, and the division between house and field slaves was drawn more tightly than it was elsewhere. This, in turn, increased resentment when planters sent house slaves to the fields as punishment, and the number of runaways increased.

The colored caste was also restive. As the children, and often the recognized children, of French fathers, they claimed equality with other children of Frenchmen. Indeed, the *code noire,* the general slave code promulgated many decades earlier, bestowed a technical equality, but new legislation took it away. French laws of the 1770s prohibited marriage of coloreds with free whites and the practice of the privileged professions, even in France.

Within the white caste, class divisions were particularly strong and class relations were bad. The planters of Saint Domingue were, more generally than elsewhere, related to the French nobility, and they were trying to raise themselves to a special privileged order equivalent to that nobility. In law, however, all colonial land was unprivileged, and colonial landowners were members of the third estate of commoners. The growing separation between the most aristocratic of the whites, called the *grands blancs,* and the others was accentuated by the bitterness of those whites who had come to the Caribbean at great personal risk to try to make a fortune but had failed. The majority of whites were still *petits blancs* – small planters, clerks, merchants' agents, shopkeepers, and skilled workers.

Relations between the colony and the metropolis created another kind of division. Officials, army officers, and merchants all had strong interests in metropolitan France; they were fully aware that their presence in the colony was temporary. The absentee planters also wanted the island to stay within the French

Empire, and so did some of the *petit blancs*. But the wealthy planters as a class found the metropolitan controls galling and would have preferred independence – all things being equal.

In the Lesser Antilles, all of these social stresses and strains were repeated, but with slightly different twists. The colonies were smaller, of course – about 85,000 slaves for each of Martinique and Guadeloupe – but with larger proportions of whites than in Saint Domingue. Economically, these islands were no longer growing rapidly. The slave trade still went on, but only to rectify the excess of deaths over births. The big growth, and the big plantations within the French sphere, were in Saint Domingue. Martinique came next in social prestige and Guadeloupe last. An eighteenth-century commentator on the French Antilles epitomized these gradations by referring to the *grand seigneurs* of Saint Domingue, the *gentillehommes* of Martinique, and the *bonnes gens* of Guadeloupe. White planters in Martinique would sometimes tell visitors, behind the hand, that all the so-called whites of Guadeloupe were really light colored people, not pure French at all.

Other social differences had economic roots. French merchants did not usually buy directly from the planters through their agents in the colonial port towns. Instead, a local class of merchants bought from individual planters, bulked the product, and sold to the French merchants. The existence of this class of brokers, or *commissaires*, helped to reduce the tension between the planters on the islands and the merchants of France, and it helped to increase the tension between the planting class on their rural estates and the townsmen and merchants with whom they dealt.

As of 1788, differences between these social tensions in the islands and those in France are immediately striking. In France, the peasantry wanted to remove the remnants of their feudal obligations. In Saint Domingue there were no peasants, only slaves; no nobles, only planters. In France the bourgeoisie resented the legal privilege of the noble estate. In Saint Domingue there was no privileged estate, only a privileged racial caste of whites who were, incidentally, members of the French third estate. In France, many wanted reform and the rationaliztion of government to make it more efficient, remove outworn abuses, and provide equality before the law. In the colony, the most vocal and powerful minorities demanded relaxation of government control, but certainly not equality – not even within the white caste, much less between white and colored. If slavery were to be considered an outworn abuse, as many people in France were beginning to believe, white colonial opinion wanted it continued as long as possible.

It is hard to see how these different social tensions would mesh together if and when revolution came in either France or Saint Domingue. Actually, they meshed in a very peculair way. When French agitators demanded change, they tended to put their particular and specific grievances in general terms. They talked about "liberty, equality, and fraternity" or about the "rights of man." The colonists saw the generalizations and read into them their own specific grievances, however different.

The *grands blancs* generally justified their attempt at separatism and their own control of the colony in terms of liberty. Clearly, they said, the general will should rule, and who, better than they, represented the general will of the colony. The *petits blancs* justified themselves in terms of fraternity, or continued union with France, the indivisible nation, in which all citizens should have an equal say. The colored people stood by the idea of equality: Were not all men (except slaves) born free and equal in their rights? Clearly they were entitled to participate as well.

The revolution on Saint Domingue

The revolution on Saint Domingue began to take form in 1788, with the first French call for a meeting of the Estates General, and it ended with Haitian independence in 1804. The events in between were most complex. One way through the maze is to envisage a drama in three acts, and with three major questions at stake: How would the colony be related to France? Who would emerge as the dominant group within the colony? What relations would that group have with the workers?

The first act of the play ran from 1788 to 1791. It was a period in which each social group with a grievance – and every social group on the island had one – entered in turn into active participation in open rebellion against someone else. The first revolt was that of the *grands blancs*. When the French government called for a meeting of the Estates General for 1789, it had not intended the colonies to be represented, but the *grands blancs* saw an opening. Here was a chance to win out over their enemies, the merchants and officials – against what they regarded as ministerial despotism and stifling trade restrictions.

They therefore elected representatives to the Estates General and sent them to France, invited or not. The representatives were mostly nobles or pseudonobles, mostly wealthy planters, and mostly from the North Province. They hung around Paris, scrapping with the absentee planters (who wanted to represent the islands themselves), and finally, by the middle of 1789, gained admission to the National Assembly. Once in Paris, curiously enough, they tended to vote with the moderate revolutionaires of the third estate.

Meanwhile, back in the colony, the same group that had sent the representatives to Paris went on to elect a set of local assemblies – one for the whole colony and one for each province. They kept the *petits blancs* out of power by limiting the franchise to those who owned twenty or more slaves, and, once elected, the assemblies began moving toward autonomy of some sort, perhaps full indpenendence following the North American precedent.

The second revolt (the second scene in the first act of the drama) was that of the *petits blancs*, the officials, and the merchants – all of whom either believed that they were being excluded from local political power or were disturbed at the prospect of colonial independence. Throughout the latter part of 1789 and early 1790, these people became increasingly agitated. Finally, in the spring of 1790, the agitation turned to civil war, though a civil war confined to the white caste; the colored people and the slaves simply looked on. The *petits blancs* were generally successful in a number of small engagements. Finally, in August 1790, the *grand blanc* Assembly of Saint Marc (in theory, the central assembly for the entire colony) captured a ship and sailed for France. The *petits blancs* had won that round, but was it a victory for the revolution or the counterrevolution? Nobody really knew. Both factions claimed to represent the revolution that was going on in France. Neither actually represented anyone but themselves – but the white civil war prepared the way for a new rising.

A third revolt, the third scene of the first act, came from the *gens de couleur*, who had not yet moved. the colored people were in a good position in France, where they could claim their equality under the rights of man. They worked through their own self-appointed representatives in Paris, cooperated with the French antislavery society – the Société des Amis des Noirs – and finally got an act passed giving them complete equality with whites throughout the French Empire. This agitation, however, took time and was not achieved until May 1791.

Meanwhile, some of the colored people preferred not to wait. One leader, Vincent Ogé, went from France to the United States, bought some arms, and landed secretly on the north coast of Saint Domingue in October 1790. He hoped to raise the colored people in a general revolt against the whites. He failed and was executed, along with several hundred others. In the end, all he accomplished was to bring about a wave of racial repression throughout the northern part of the island. That was the final revolt of the first act of the drama. By the summer of 1791, all the possible white and colored factions had entered the revolution. All claimed to be revolutionary and against the Old Regime. All claimed to represent the ideals of the revolution in France.

The second act began when the slaves moved. They had done nothing significant during the three years of disputation that had begun in mid-1788. Small-scale slave rebellions had occurred throughout the seventeenth and early eighteenth centuries. Runaway bands of maroons were already in the hills, especially the mountain chain separating the French from the Spanish part of the islands. All they needed was an opportunity, and the struggles between the white and colored factions supplied one.

The rebellion broke out in August 1791. Within ten days the whole North Province was in revolt, leaving the whites only a weak hold on the city of Cap Français itself. Within the first month about 200 sugar estates had been burned, along with many more coffee and other small plantations. About 1,000 whites were caught in rural areas and killed. The rest escaped to the towns, and many left the island.

The successful surprise of the revolt shows the organizational ability of the leadership. It was one thing to organize a revolt in secret that could carry one or two plantations. This one carried the greater part of the North Province at one time. The exact nature of that organization is unknown and unknowable at this distance in time. Given the size of the operation, the leaders must have been drawn from among the existing leaders of the slave society. On eighteenth-century plantations, slave leaders were either trained, skilled slaves who had learned a good deal about European culture – slave drivers whom the others were already accustomed to obey – or people with significant roles in the traditional religion.

The original leader of the North Province revolt of 1791, for example, was a *commandeur de plantation,* the equivalent of a head driver. He was also a cult leader in a non-Christian religious sect of a type ancestral to the modern Haitian vodun. The French records report his name as Boukman. Boukman was the title of a quasi-religious, quasi-political officer in some Mande or Malinké states in West Africa at that time. The coincidence may not indicate that the leader was himself African born, but it suggests that his leadership had religious roots in Haitian creole culture. Boukman may have been his title rather than his name.

This second act of the drama of revolution lasted from August 1791 well into 1794. It was marked by generalized anarchy, civil war, and swift changes in the fortunes of those wars. It was, in essence, a four-sided civil war among the two white factions, the colored, and the slaves acting in various combinations. In 1793, Spanish forces from the other half of the island and British forces from Jamaica also joined in, so that the fighting became six-sided. A six-sided war is hard to fight consistently; temporary alliances and combinations tend to emerge; chance and circumstance made for strange bedfellows.

As an example, toward the end of 1791, three different forms of alliance existed simultaneously in the three provinces. In the North Province, the slave rising posed such a threat that the whites and coloreds forgot their differences and joined forces to protect Cap Français. In the West Province there was still no slave rising, but the planting class as a whole (both white and colored) was so unfriendly to the officials, *petits blancs,* and merchants of Port-au-Prince that the struggle became a rural–urban conflict – caste and race aside. In the South Province, coffee planters had better relations with their slaves than was the case elsewhere in the island but the white–colored conflict was very bitter. In this area, some of the white and colored planters armed their slaves and fought each other in a war between the two upper castes, the slaves taking part on both sides. Here the townsmen, who were few in any case, played only a minor part.

But none of these situations could be permanent. During 1792 the slave revolt spread to the two southern provinces. Anarchy became general. From then on, the only overall leadership came from the commissioners sent out from France. These commissioners, in effect governors, were the representatives of revolutionary France. They tried to decide which, if any, of the various groups in the colonial society were the true equivalents of the *sans culottes,* the lower ranks of the bourgeoisie, who were becoming more powerful in the National Assembly throughout 1793 and 1794.

They tried, at first, to form an alliance of *petits blancs* and colored people, since neither the big planters nor the slaves seemed much like good French bourgeois. This alliance was never strong, but it could work as long as the slaves were the greatest threat to any part of the old order. But the course of military affairs brought about some important shifts. The slave forces weakened, and the British and Spanish invaders became more of a threat. In this situation, some *grands blancs* in 1793 thought they saw the opportunity for a cout d'etat against the French officials. In response, the officials were forced to seek support further down in the colonial class structure. They responded by arming some 12,000 slaves, who became their main fighting force, capable of holding whatever part of the island France held at all.

Then, in 1794, the National Assembly in France shifted further to the left. It proclaimed the emancipation of the slaves in all the colonies. With this, the leaders of the ex-slaves in rebellion against France on Saint Domingue changed sides. The French commissioners could then rally the support of the ex-slaves as a group. That ended the second act with a victory for the slaves (in the struggle for local superiority) and for France (in the struggle between the colony and the metropolis).

The third act occupied the entire decade of 1794 to 1804. It was an equally confused period in which the slave victory was mainly assured; but the French victory was nullified, and Haiti emerged as an independent state. This shift in Haitain affairs was mainly the work of Toussaint L'Ouverture. He was one of the many slave

leaders who had fought on one side, then another. The Emancipation Act brought him to the side of France in the summer of 1794.
From then on, he built a growing following among the black group
as a whole. With this unity he was able to defeat first the British
and Spanish invaders, then the remaining *gens de couleur*, and
finally the governor-general sent from France to take control of the
newly won colony. By 1801, Toussaint was in actual contol, and he
was recognized by France as the official representative of French
power.

Perhaps this really is the end of the drama, but with an epilogue.
In 1802 and 1803 the French tried to reconquer the colony, but
failed. They captured Toussaint L'Ouverture and sent him to
France. The final defense of his work was left to his lieutenants,
Jean-Jacques Desallines and Henri Christophe. By 1803, they had
driven out the French. On January 1, 1804, they proclaimed the
independence of Haiti.

Other islands, other combinations

The French Revolution in the Lesser Antilles differed in detail, but
not in the possible patterns of revolt. The beginning was much as
it had been in Saint Domingue. Planters moved first, sending their
delegates to the Estates General to complain about imperial
economic controls and to demand greater autonomy. As on Saint
Domingue, the entrance of each new faction created new combinations.

On Martinique in 1790, the local tensions between the planting
class and the townsmen in general became so important that they
turned into a rural–urban civil war. In this instance, both factions
armed their slaves, who then fought on both sides. The colored
people, however, took the side of the great planters, some of
whom were their relatives, and opposed their economic competitors, the *petit blanc* townsmen. It was, in short, a near-repetition of
the situation in the West Province of Saint Domingue in 1791–2,
but on Martinique no slave revolt intervened. The civil war went
on until 1794, when the British captured the island, ending the
revolution once and for all.

On Guadeloupe, the situation was different. The *bonnes gens*
lived up to their reputation for easy race relations between white

and colored. With peace among the upper strata, the slaves stayed in place as well. Then came the British invasion of 1794. Revolutionary France counterattacked under Commissioner Victor Hugues, who raised the slaves in rebellion against the British and the local planters alike. The slave–French alliance won in the first instance and drove out the British. In this sense, Guadeloupe in 1794 went directly to the situation of Saint Domingue at the same date – without the preliminaries.

From then on, the revolution in the Lesser Antilles was only a minor theme in the Anglo–French war for empire. The British recaptured Guadeloupe in 1796; the French returned in 1802 and reimposed slavery. With the peace of 1815, France reimposed slavery in all the sugar islands still under French control, with a substantial renewed slave trade throughout the 1820s and again, in disguised form, in the 1850s. In 1848, however, legal slavery was finally abolished in the French Empire. Thus, with a half-century delay, the plantation complex that collapsed in Saint Domingue in the 1790s finally ended for the French Empire as a whole.

Suggestions for further reading

Geggus, David, *Slavery, War, and Revolution: The British Occuaption of Saint Domingue 1793–1798* (Oxford: Clarendon Press, 1982).

Pérotin-Dumon, Anne, *Etre patriote sous les tropiques: La Guadeloupe, la colonisation, et la révolution (1789–1794)* (Basseterre: Société d'histoire de la Guadeloupe, 1985).

Aftermath

13

Readjustments in the nineteenth century

The beginning of the end of the plantation complex is correctly associated with the Democratic Revolution. The full liquidation of the complex was a longer process extending through the nineteenth century and into the twentieth. It had grown by adding one feature after another; it came apart by dropping one after another. Even when legal slavery ended, plantations often continued as the dominant economic unit – still managed by people of mainly European descent, still worked by people of mainly African descent. Even the old work organization of gang labor under intense supervision continued on some Caribbean islands into the twentieth century. After slavery ended, other forms of coercion continued – debt peonage, contract labor with penal sanctions, vagrancy laws, or regressive taxation aimed at forcing peasants to become wage laborers in order to meet the demands of the tax collector.

In spite of these holdovers, the nineteenth century brought fundamental changes throughout the world economy. Some were clear consequences of industrialism. Others were more nearly the long-run results of much older processes in world history. A fundamental demographic change was one of these. The plantation complex and the slave trade had been linked by net natural decrease in plantation populations. The slave population of the United States began to grow by natural increase in the eighteenth century. During the nineteenth century, one tropical plantation society after another passed from net natural decrease to population growth – often at explosive rates. Barbados achieved a self-sustaining slave population about 1805, followed by the other British West Indian colonies in the next fifty years or so. By the second half of the century, Barbados and Jamaica, among others, began sending emigrants to Panama, Cuba, the United States, and ultimately Europe.[1] Haiti, over the centuries from the 1780s to the 1980s, passed from being one of the greatest labor importers of the slave-trade era to overpopulation and poverty, with far too many people for its limited resources.

The end of the slave trade

English writers in the nineteenth century made a convenient distinction between the *abolition* of the slave trade and the *emancipation* of the slaves. These were, indeed, the two legal acts that ended the plantation complex. In retrospect, they appear as an automatic sequence, but the linkage appeared less automatic at the time. Even a slaveholder could favor abolition of the trade in the hope of preventing slave-based competition from new colonies. In the United States, the slave regime continued to flourish economically down to the 1860s, even though slave imports had been cut off early in the nineteenth century.

The end of the slave trade had both European and extra-European roots. In Europe, abolitionism became part of the broad ideology of the Democratic Revolution expressed through the British and Foreign Anti-Slavery Society or the Société des Amis des Noirs. Their battles were fought and won through the press, Parliament, and the National Assembly. In the European forum, the sequence of events is reasonably neat, beginning in the 1780s with the moral condemnation of the trade, reaching legislative abolition in Britain, the Netherlands, Denmark, and the United States before 1810. After 1815, one by one, the other powers made the trade illegal, however little they did to put a stop to it in practice. Britain, with belated help from France and the United States, took more forceful action with a blockade of the West African coast. It was only partially successful, but in 1850 Brazil began enforcing its own laws against slave imports and that

---

[1] George W. Roberts, *The Population of Jamaica* (Cambridge: Cambridge University Press, 1957).

market was effectively closed. After 1865, transatlantic slave shipments were only sporadic. The Atlantic slave trade was dead.

On the colonial side, the fundamental changes were economic and demographic, but the territories that were demographically mature were not always those with immediate potential for economic development. In the United States in the early nineteenth century, westward expansion of the Cotton Kingdom meant westward migration of planters and slaves. In the Caribbean, some British colonies, like Barbados, appeared to be overpopulated, whereas others newly acquired during the Napoleonic Wars – like Trinidad and British Guiana – lacked population for further development. Cuba was just beginning its own sugar revolution in the early nineteenth century, and central Brazilian provinces like São Paulo and Rio de Janeiro were opening frontiers for sugar and coffee. Brazil and Cuba tried to keep the slave trade going as long as possible, but other sugar colonies looked elsewhere.

New migrations: new wine in old bottles

Even before the legal end of the African slave trade, some planters began to shift to India as an alternative source. As early as the 1780s, planters in the Mascarene Islands – Mauritius and Réunion – had imported a few slaves from India. With the return of international peace in 1815, humanitarian sentiment and the end of the African slave trade made an overt return to a slave trade difficult. Migration with a labor contract, however, could be made to seem more humanitarian. The contract was, after all, similar to the indentures that servants for the Antilles had once signed in Britain itself. In the early nineteenth century, redemptionists with similar obligations were still brought from Europe to the United States.

A regular system of contract labor was therefore organized with the cooperation of the government of British India. The labor recruit in India signed a contract to migrate and work in a plantation colony for a period of years – three, five, sometimes ten. At the end of that time, the worker was usually entitled to return transportation, though comparatively few received it. Once freed of the contract, most found themselves in a country with a continuing labor shortage. They had signed the contract in the first place mainly because their economic and social position in India was so bad that almost anything seemed to be an improvement.

Historians have wondered whether contract labor was in fact a new form a slavery. It certainly was a form of coerced labor – usually as unpleasant for the worker as slavery itself, but not identical to the old system. The contractor could sell the laborer's contract to a third party without his consent. The contract was also enforceable by penal sanctions. If the worker refused to work, the state would step in with the ultimate threat of prison at hard labor. Physical punishment with the whip was not usually legal, but it was very common; the other conditions of slavery were all present – except the permanence of the servitude. Contract workers were also paid a small wage – admittedly far below the market rate – and those in the West Indies had better protection against personal abuse, through recourse to the courts, than the slaves had ever had.

Both the British and the French developed schemes for the more or less coerced emigration from Africa to the West Indies. In the 1840s, the British set out to encourage "voluntary" emigration from Africa. Slaves recaptured at sea were usually landed at Sierra Leone, because it was too hard to return them to their countries of origin. Recaptives in Sierra Leone or Saint Helena were urged to sign five-year indentures for the West Indies. Only about 15,000 actually made the trip before the scheme was dropped as both expensive and inhumane.

In the 1850s, the French had an even more obvious scheme for "free" emigration from Africa. They bought slaves on the African coast, legally emancipated them on the spot, and then shipped them off to the Antilles as theoretically free contract workers for a period of time, though the "free immigrants" had no choice in the matter. About 15,000 reached the West Indies by this route.

In all, between 1845 and 1914, India supplied nearly 450,000 contract workers for the British West Indies. It also supplied contract workers for the French Caribbean. The Dutch drew on the Javanese for the plantations in Surinam, and Cuba imported about 150,000 Chinese contract workers between 1849 and 1875. Meanwhile, Cuba and Puerto Rico together imported about 600,000 slaves from Africa between 1811 and 1870. For the Caribbean as a whole, in short, the number of non-African coerced laborers imported in the nineteenth century slightly exceeded the number of Africans who still came in by way of the illegal slave trade.

The end of slavery in the French and British Caribbean

Like the abolition of the slave trade, the emancipation of the slaves was partly an offshoot of the Democratic Revolution in Europe, supported by local pressure in the colonies – some from the slaves themselves, but also from local opponents of slavery, among whom missionaries and the free colored people were the most prominent. Pressure from the *gens de couleur* was especially important in the French colonies, but in either set of colonies they were crucial. Their numbers grew steadily from natural increase. As the old sugar islands lost prosperity, many members of the old white ruling class tended to drift "home" to Europe. The colored had no other home and they often played key roles, representing the interests of the slaves and the emancipated ex-slaves, though they sometimes tried to guard their own position of superiority over the freedmen.

Just as emancipation in the British colonies followed parliamentary reform at home, steps toward French emancipation followed the main phases of political change in Europe. With the revolution of 1830 and the July Monarchy in Paris, the *gens de couleur* were enfranchised in the French Antilles. With the Revolution of 1848, the National Assembly emancipated the remaining slaves and extended manhood suffrage even to the ex-slaves – finally making good the promise of emancipation first enacted in 1794.

Economic change was sometimes another factor encouraging emancipation. As the sugar industry moved on to new ground, the old sugar colonies suffered from the competition. Cuba and Puerto Rico had the clean-slate advantage combined with new and fertile land to work. The Antilles as a whole suffered from the new production in Cuba and sometimes in Brazil. Within the British tariff system, Jamaica and the other British West Indies suffered from new production in British Guiana, Trinidad, and Mauritius. The French Antilles suffered from new production using Indian labor on Réunion. Economic depression in some of these older colonies removed certain incentives to keep the old labor system going in the face of political pressure.

Individual colonies took their own paths to readjustment. Some, like Barbados, kept on with the plantation regime, using free labor. Others abandoned sugar for new exports like bananas or nutmeg. In others, like Jamaica, many of the large plantations failed and the land was broken up for sale to smallholders, who supported themselves on a few acres, growing cash crops like bananas, nutmeg, pimento, or allspice, along with tree or root crops like breadfruit, manioc, and akee for local consumption.

New plantations: old wine in new bottles

The industrial age brought new wealth to Europe, and new wealth meant new demand for tropical products. Sugar had once been a luxury only the rich could afford. In 1700, the per capita consumption in Britain was only about 4 pounds a year; by the 1750s, it had doubled. Over the next fifty years, per capita sugar consumption doubled again, reaching 18 pounds by 1800 or a little later. There it stabilized for a time, but in the late 1840s the British removed the sugar duties, dropping the price to consumers by about half, and consumption per capita more than doubled. By the mid-twentieth century, however, sugar had become so cheap, compared to incomes in advanced industrial societies, that almost all persons ate as much as they wanted, regardless of price. Price may still guide the choice between different sources of sugar – cane, beet, maize, and so on – but the final level of sugar consumption in developed countries tends to be about 100 pounds per capita per year, plus or minus 20 pounds, depending on local taste.

Growing European prosperity in the nineteenth century brought new demand for other tropical crops – coffee from Java and the West Indies at first, then from Brazil, Colombia, and Ceylon; tea from Assam in northeastern India; and finally, before the end of the century, rubber fron Malaysia. This new demand set the sugar industry moving once more – within the Caribbean, but elsewhere as well. The Mascarene Islands were a major new source. Mauritius was not far from India, the new source of labor; in the early nineteenth century, its sugar production rose faster than that of any other British colony. The colony of Natal in South Africa also developed a new sugar industry – also based on labor from India, coerced labor in this case moving to Africa, not away from it. Far away in the Pacific, Fiji's new sugar industry drew in so many Indian sugar workers that more than half of the present population is of Indian descent.

Nor was India the only new source of coerced plantation labor. Queensland in northern Australia used Melanesian Pacific islanders, recruited through force or fraud by "blackbirders" who sailed the southwestern Pacific looking for workers. A new sugar industry in the irrigated valleys of coastal Peru used Chinese labor, with conditions at least as bad as those of Caribbean slavery. Even Hawaii under the monarchy, before annexation by the United States, imported workers from China and Japan under contracts with penal sanctions.

Just as mining in Brazil and new Granada had drawn in labor from the slave trade, new mining enterprises in the nineteenth century used contract labor, just as the plantations did. Chinese capitalists had operated tin mines in Malaya long before the colonial period began; but European industrialization increased the world demand for tin, and contract labor from South China met the need for labor in the tin mines.

In past migrations of the sugar industry, managers and skilled workers carried the techniques and mores from the old plantations to the new. In the nineteenth century, sugar masters from the Caribbean carried the technology and style of management to the new plantations in Africa and Asia. In the first stage, they helped to set up the industry in Mauritius, Natal, and Queensland. Later, these secondary centers became sources for an even wider spread of technology. Technicians and managers from the Caribbean had their own mental image of what a plantation should be and how it should be run. Their model was the slave plantation, and their background included a belief in European racial superiority, ideas about labor discipline, and concepts of a proper social order. Though the slave plantation was being phased out in the Caribbean, aspects of the plantation complex spread far and wide throughout the tropical world.

Older histories of the Americas describe a declining slave trade not compensated for by the new flow of immigrants from Asia. That picture is correct when it concentrates on the Caribbean alone. The total movement of Indian workers to non-Asian destinations came to about a million emigrants between 1834 and 1916, or an annual average about a third of the size of the Atlantic slave trade from Africa at its peak. But that total neglects the worldwide spread of the plantation complex in the nineteenth century. Most Indian contract workers moved within Asia – to places like Ceylon, Assam, Burma, and Malaysia. If these destinations are taken into account, outward movement of Indian workers was certainly greater than departures from sub-Saharan Africa at the peak of the slave trade.

Chinese population exports of the nineteenth century are less well known, but counting the massive movement into Southeast Asia, Chinese emigration at this period was even greater than that from India. The decline of the Atlantic slave trade, in short, was balanced by a substantially larger population movement from Asia. Some of these people went to sugar plantations on the old model; but many went to new kinds of plantations producing a much wider range of crops, and some went to mining and other kinds of work, in much the same way that earlier migration from Africa had spilled over to serve other needs in the Americas.

African adjustments

From the beginning of the end of the legal slave trade in 1808 to 1865, Africa stopped exporting people and began exporting other products. In the language of time, it substituted "legitimate trade" for the slave trade, but the process was far from simple. The period from about 1780 to 1880 is sometimes known in African history as the "precolonial century." It saw the end of the slave trade, but new influences from industrializing Europe were equally important, and it ended with the European conquests.

Even the ending of the slave trade brought more European influence, not less. The slave trade had rarely brought European navies to African waters, but the British campaign against the slave trade at sea did. The simple availability of power changed relations between European traders and their African trade partners. In the past, they had functioned as near-equals, but now the Europeans were in a postion to call in the navy. The British also took the lead in establishing consuls at key points on the African coast, with specific orders to interfere in neighboring African states. Initially, they intervened to help suppress the slave trade, but other issues inevitably entered the picture.

New power furthered the spread of Western influence, already begun in the eighteenth century. During the period of the slave trade, Afro-European communities had grown up around the main slave trade posts – Portuguese in Luanda and Mozambique; Dutch, English, and Danish of the Gold Coast; French at the mouth of the Senegal River. These trading towns advanced cultural exchange in both directions. Some Europeans accepted African culture, married African wives, and founded important African trading families.

By the late eighteenth century, African slave dealers sometimes sent their sons or other dependents to England, France, or Holland for education – not often at the university level, but long enough to master a European language and European commercial practices. Once literate, they continued to use the European language for their own commercial records and occasionally for other writings. Not many of these African records in Western languages have survived the physical decay of a tropical climate, but an eighteenth-century diary kept by an African slave dealer from Calabar in eastern Nigeria was discovered in Scotland and published.[2]

In the 1790s, the British had a small colony at Sierra Leone, originally settled by black poor from London, loyalist Afro-Americans, and exiled maroons from Jamaica. When the British began to capture illegal slavers at sea, Sierra Leone was a convenient place to unload them. Antislavery enthusiasts helped to make Sierra Leone an early center for missionary work and for Western-style education, not simply for the elite but for the mass of slaves recaptured at sea – at least at an elementary level. Similar, if less intense, French activity around Saint Louis in Senegal produced a significant group of Western-educated Africans there as well.

By midcentury, a Western-educated African elite had come into existence, scattered up and down the West African coast. It included a Catholic abbé from Senegal and an Anglican bishop

---

[2] The diary of Entera Duke, published in C. Dayll Forde (ed.), *Efik Trders of Old Calabar* (London: Oxford University Press, 1956).

who had originally been a Yoruba slave boy recaptured at sea. Others were missionaries and journalists and doctors, some of them Afro-Americans or West Indian returnees to freed-slave settlements like those at Sierra Leone or Liberia.

By the 1860s and 1870s, some of these people began to work for further westernization – culture change on the initiative of the borrowing culture, not just that of the missionaries. What this West African movement toward modernization might have amounted to, were it not for the European conquests that began in the 1880s, is hard to predict. Several West African initiatives, however, can at least serve as straws in the wind.

Some of the modernizers tried to form new states or to change old ones by borrowing Western political models. On the Gold Coast in the early 1870s, it appeared that Britain might withdraw from the coastal forts. Western-educated officials and merchants began to work with traditional chiefs to create a new Fante Confederation uniting the micro-states along the coast. These states would otherwise have been at the mercy of Asante power in their hinterland. The new Fante constitution called for a representative government to share power between the chiefs and the educated elite. Some of the Ga-speaking people around Accra made a similar attempt with a short-lived Republic of Accra. Both the Republic of Accra and the Fante Confederation collapsed, however, when Britain decided not to evacuate its posts after all.

In 1865, next door in what was to be Nigeria, still another group of westernized Africans joined traditional authorities to found the Egba United Board of Management in the Yoruba city-state of Abeokuta. The board was to act as a governing body, dividing power between the new elite and the old, not unlike the Fante Confederation. The result was not without friction between the two groups, and with British officials in nearby Lagos as well. The formal movement did not last, but Abeokuta was able to struggle on and to retain its formal independence until 1914.

All three of these examples lay beyound direct European control, but other modernizing Africans chose to work within the European sphere, in the trade forts and their vicinity. Returned slaves from Brazil and their descendants became an important commercial group in western Nigeria and the Republic of Bénin. Other Africans worked closely with the European authorities as missionaries and as medical doctors in the colonial service. Several men of mixed Afro-European descent held important posts in the colonial government – as the acting governor of the Gold Coast, the commander of a French expedition to the upper Senegal, or the commander of the French forces in the conquest of Dahomey (now the Republic of Bénin).

The politics and economics of legitimate trade

On the economic side, the end of the Atlantic slave trade was more complex than simple abolition might make it appear. Many slaves had been a by-product of warfare, and warfare went on even after the overseas market dried up. During the century between about 1780 and 1880, Africa was more anarchic and disorderly than it had been before 1780 – not less so. Religious revolutions with a purified Islam as a goal changed political frontiers throughout the western Sudan and into the forest zone along the coast. Beginning in 1804, Usuman dan Fodio rebelled against the less than pious secular leaders in Hausaland. Within a decade his followers had created the caliphate of Sokoto, uniting much of the present northern Nigeria and parts of neighboring Niger. A similar movement on the middle Niger, in what is now Mali, created the caliphate of Hamdallahi.

In the second half of the century, still another religious leader, Shaykh Umar Tal, conquered a large territory along the sahel between the Senegal and Timbuktu at the Niger bend, then south into the upper part of present-day Guinea-Conakry. To the south of Shaykh Umar's empire, Samori Turé conquered a belt of territory about 150 miles wide, stretching from Kankan in Guinea-Conakry east into northern Ghana.

All this empire building involved fighting. Fighting bred enslavement, and the supply of slaves exceeded the local demand. They became cheaper than ever before at the point of capture. A century or so earlier, a captor might receive, in real terms, the value of food to sustain a slave for ten to fifteen years. In the wars of Samori, slaves were sometimes sold for the value of a week's maintenance. Merchants followed the armies to buy the newly enslaved; but export by sea was closed, and they had to be sold in other parts of Africa.

After the mid-nineteenth century and the end of the export slave trade, foreign exchange earnings from this source were certainly reduced. The distribution of income within western Africa also changed. Lower prices for slaves at the point of capture meant that captors received less. Those merchants who specialized in the trade to the coast either lost out or went into another branch of commerce. Political authorities on the main trade routes had grown rich taxing the passing caravans. They lost out as well unless they were lucky enough to find new currents of taxable legitimate trade passing through their territory.

Yet even before the slave trade tapered off, legitimate trade began to take its place. New foreign exchange earned by these new exports more than balanced the loss of the slave exports, but the profits from new trade often went to different people. Whereas the slave trade in its last decades had drawn captives from areas ever deeper in the interior, new products for export orginated closer to the coasts. Some of these products – gold, hides, gum arabic, wax, ivory, timber, and dye woods – had been exported for centuries, but the quantities increased enormously in the nineteenth century, driven by increased European demand.

Industrialization in Europe also created new kinds of demand, especially for fats and oils. Before petroleum products were available, vegetable and animal fats and oils served for lubrication, nutrition, soap making, and even illumination. For tropical Africa, the new demand encouraged the production of peanut oil in the savanna zone. From the coast and the forest belt it called for copra, palm oil, and palm kernels.

The role of European traders remained what it had been in the era of the slave trade. They appeared on the coast, announcing their readiness to buy; Africans responded by producing the goods and bringing them to the coast for sale. The only technological innovation was the steamboat, which became important on the Senegal River from the 1820s, and on the lower Niger and its tributaries from the 1850s.

Many Europeans hoped for another kind of economic development in Africa – for tropical plantations under European management. Development planners began to think of Africa as an alternative and supplement to West Indian production, since the Caribbean was unable to keep up with the new demand for

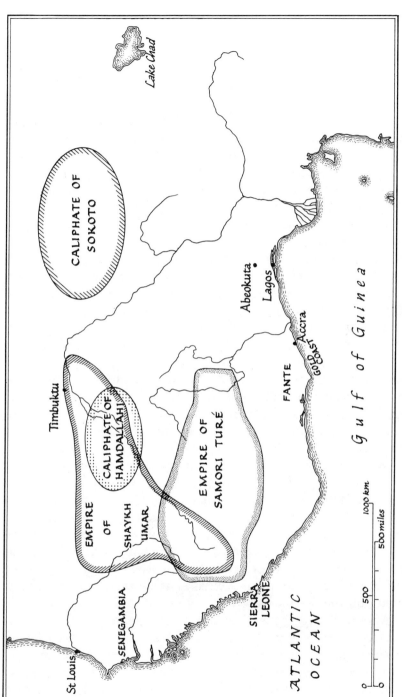

Figure 13.1 West Africa in the nineteenth century.

tropical staples. Historians often give little space to plans that failed, but they are important to show intentions, if not achievements. The founders of Sierra Leone hoped to set up something like a wage labor variant of St. Kitts or an equivalent sugar colony. British capitalists in the 1790s also occupied the island of Bolama, now in Guinea-Bissau, with the same goal. In fact, Sierra Leone never produced sugar for export, and the would-be founders of Bolama died of malaria and yellow fever.

Even these lessons were lost. After the French reoccupied their old post at the mouth of the Senegal in 1817, they tried to turn the riverbank into a plantation colony to replace their lost colony of Saint Domingue, and they too failed. Later, in 1841–2, the British government sent a major expedition up the Niger River by steamboat, hoping to develop model plantations so as to encourage the African authorities to take up the example. Some of the planners were humanitarians who hoped to strike a blow at North American slavery by turning to Africa for cotton. They hoped that Britain would lose its dangerous dependence on American cotton and that the economic collapse of the Cotton Kingdom in the American South would lead to slave emancipation in the United States. The expedition even took along an Afro-American specialist in cotton cultivation to teach the Africans how to take care of the crop. But the plan failed before it could get off the ground. Most of the Europeans on the expedition died of malaria within weeks, and the steamboats had to be withdrawn.

Instead, Afro-European commercial relations continued as they had grown up in the era of the slave trade. The transition was especially successful at the Niger Delta, where old trading towns like Nembe, Bonny, Kalabari – and Calabar, farther east on the Cross River – used the existing trade networks into the interior, first to supply palm oil as well as slaves. But, as the slave trade died out, the oil trade grew.

After about 1860, new troubles began. Steamers had begun to use the Niger River. This meant that the old-style traders lost business to new European firms able to buy directly from the producers along the river. To make matters worse, the price of palm oil began to fall, while that of European manufactures rose;

the terms of trade that had been shifting in West Africa's favor for nearly a century began to turn the other way.

Here, as elsewhere, changing times distributed income in new ways. One kind of change affected African politics. Political authorities who controlled coastal points and the trade routes had profited enormously from the slave trade. They had few direct expenses; their net profit from the price paid for slaves at the point of export was therefore greater than that of either the initial captors or the merchants who traveled the trade routes. When the export slave trade declined, merchants could shift to new products over new routes; political authorities could not. As they lost income, they often lost power as well. The result was an increase in political disorganization, though with great variation from one kingdom to the next. Over the century from 1780 to 1880, however, it is fair to say that the old political elite lost both power and wealth; or else it entered trade on its own account in order to profit from the new channels of commerce.

In a number of the larger West African states – Asante, Bénin, and Dahomey, for example – the old leadership held on, neither losing out nor adjusting to the new possibilities of economic growth. It held most of its power, indeed, until the 1890s, when these countries fell to the European invaders. In Senegambia, on the other hand, the secular leadership tried to keep up its former level of income by making new demands on the peasantry. From the 1850s through the 1870s, the peasants rose in revolt under the leadership of Muslim clerics. The clerics wanted reform for their own religious reasons, but they accepted the help they could get. They won power in one kingdom after another until, in the 1880s and 1890s, it was they, and not the former secular chiefs, who went down fighting the European conquest.

The abolition of the slave trade and the emancipation of the slaves forced both the former slave buyers and the former slave sellers to readjust to new conditions. Both were caught up in a new pace of historical change based on the new industrial growth. No sooner had they met one crisis than another was on them. The final act for Africa was European conquest. For the old plantations of the Caribbean, it was an immense expansion of the planting regime to the whole of the tropical world, leaving the old sugar colonies in a comparative backwater. For Brazil and Cuba, it was to bring on the final steps in the revolution of slave emancipation.

Suggestions for further reading

Curtin, Philip D., *Two Jamaicas* (Cambridge: Harvard University Press, 1955). *The Image of Africa* (Madison: University of Wisconsin Press, 1964).

Drescher, Seymour, *Econocide: British Slavery in the Era of Abolition* (Pittsburgh: University of Pittsburgh Press, 1977).

Davis, David Brion, *The Problem of Slavery in Western Culture* (Ithaca: Cornell University Press, 1966).

Eltis, David, *Economic Growth and the Ending of the Transatlantic Slave Trade* (New York: Oxford University Press, 1987).

Eltis, David, and James Walvin (eds.), *The Abolition of the Atlantic Slave Trade: Origins and Effects in Europe, Africa, and the Americas* (Madison: University of Wisconsin Press, 1981).

Green, William, *British Slave Emancipation: The Sugar Colonies and the Great Experiment 1830–1865* (Oxford: Clarendon Press, 1976).

July, Robert, *The Origins of Modern African Thought: Its Development in West Africa During the Nineteenth and Twentieth Centuries* (New York: Praeger, 1967).

Schuler, Monica, *"Alas, Alas, Kongo": A Social History of Indentured Immigration into Jamaica, 1841–1865* (Baltimore: Johns Hopkins University Press, 1980).

Tinker, Hugh, *A New System of Slavery: The Export of Indian Labour Overseas 1830–1920* (London: Oxford University Press, 1974).

14

The end of slavery in the Americas

The end of slavery in Cuba and Brazil was out of phase with emancipation elsewhere. It came nearly a century later than the slave revolt in Saint Domingue, a half-century after the emancipation of the slaves in the British Empire, four decades after the final abolition of slavery in the French colonies, and a little more than twenty years after the end of slavery in the United States and of serfdom in Russia. One question is: Why did slavery last so much longer here than it did in many larger societies that were more important on the world scene?

In fact, the timing was not so different. The dates of the formal legal emancipation create a misconception. Emancipation in Saint Domingue was an atypcial event, set off by the French Revolution. The French themselves rescinded their Emancipation Act of 1794 once Napoleon was safely in power. British, American, and French emancipations, formally declared between the 1830s and the 1860s, still preserved racial domination, and institutions like Indian contract labor helped to preserve the reality of the plantation complex into the twentieth century. During these same decades, both Cuba and Brazil had begun to dismantle their own slave systems. The Emancipation Act of 1833 for the British Empire, in effect, marked the beginning of a process of liquidating slavery, and the emancipation acts in Brazil and Cuba in the late 1880s came near the end of the same process in those countries.

Historians have discussed slave emancipation under the shadow of a debate over the primacy of humanitarian or economic motives. Was slavery ended because it was morally wrong or because it was unprofitable? The issue is not usually put that starkly, and each act of emancipation has its own body of literature arguing either side of the question. A general answer for all acts of emancipation in the nineteenth century may not be possible. It is not, in any event, practical to enter the debate at that level of generalization, though historians have recently argued that slavery was an economically viable set of institutions – to the slave owners and to the economy of the principal slaveholding regions – at the time it was abolished. But that hardly counts, if – as in the United States – those who forced emancipation on the slave owners were acting for a larger political unit in which the interests of the slave owners were not dominant.

In Cuba and Brazil, the slave economies were also profitable at the time of emancipation – at least to most of the slave owners. Emancipation was forced on them by an alliance of other interests within each country, and to some degree by international pressure from the most advanced industrial countries of the time, especially Great Britain, France, and the United States, which had already abolished slavery within their own spheres.

Brazil: sugar and coffee

As a geographical entity, the Brazil of the nineteenth century was not the same as the Brazil of the sixteenth or seventeenth. The Brazil of the early plantation complex was the northeast, and only narrow coastal sectors at that. Though the northeast gained from the opening of the British market to foreign sugar in 1846, the northeastern plantations were technically outmoded, and they soon lost out to competition from new plantations in Cuba, from beet sugar in Europe, and even from new plantations in other parts of Brazil. The new sugar industry in Brazil was along the central coast, especially in the province of Rio de Janeiro, but it developed quite late in the century – in the 1870s and after – and it was overshadowed within Brazil by the spectacular rise of coffee planting.

The new coffee industry was in São Paulo, Rio de Janeiro, and Minas Gerais – the provinces usually lumped together as the south-central region. Coffee alone was important enough to *plantation complex linked to slave trade & slavery.*

account for the entire increase in Brazil's foreign trade in the first half of the nineteenth century. New agricultural enterprises on new ground brought the usual demand for imported labor – met in the usual way, through the slave trade, at least until the 1850s. Brazil imported an annual average of 37,000 slaves a year between 1811 and 1850 – more than two-thirds of the Atlantic slave trade of that period. About 70 percent of this total went directly to Rio de Janeiro or Santos (the port for São Paulo), though many slaves first landed elsewhere and were later transferred to the south-central region.

Even after the 1850s, when Brazil began to enforce its anti-slave-trade legislation, the internal slave trade continued, drawing labor from the northeast toward the south-central provinces in response to slave prices there that had trebled by 1880. Recent estimates put this stream of slaves in the vicinity of 5,000 to 6,000 a year between 1850 and the emancipation of the last Brazilian slaves in 1888.

External pressure to end the slave trade and slavery came principally from Great Britain. It was partly diplomatic, backed by potential economic sanctions and Britain's naval action to suppress the trade at sea. Behind that pressure lay the same intellectual and moral concerns that had already led to abolition and emancipation elsewhere. In nineteenth century Brazil and Cuba, two other themes were important. One was the accusation that the slave trade was not only immoral, it was unworthy of a civilized nation. This may seem inconsequential, but it was important to Cuban and Brazilian opinion. Cuba, Spain, and Brazil were far down the line in comparative economic development and power among the Western nations. They were dependent on the more developed countries both materially and intellectually; some of their people resented this dependence and wanted to catch up.

Western racism was a second theme. It had grown in intensity during the first half of the century and was still growing. By the 1880s, pseudoscientific racism was an accepted doctrine of Western science. But the relationship of racism to the slavery question was not the same in Brazil and Cuba as it was in the United States on the eve of the Civil War. In the United States, racism, claiming the inferiority of Afro-Americans, was a defense

Brazil's inferiority complex.

of slavery. In Brazil, it could be used to oppose slavery. If Africans were racially inferior, the argument went, to continue the slave trade was to increase the "inferiority" of Brazilian society; and the slave trade discouraged potential immigration of "superior" people from Europe. After abolition, similar arguments were used to favor emancipation. If slavery discouraged European immigration, it prevented the "whitening" of the Brazilian population and hence the "improvement" of the Brazilian gene pool. In spite of these and similar arguments, internal pressure for emancipation began to build up only in the 1870s. The Brazilian Anti-Slavery Society was not founded until 1880.

Brazil's first significant move toward emancipation came with the Rio Branco Law of 1871. It was passed under pressure from France, and with the slave owners' hope that an appearance of reform might stave off still stronger pressure from overseas. An older interpretation of Brazilian history insisted that the Brazilians and Portuguese were less racist than other Europeans. It went on to praise Brazilian slave owners for emancipating many slaves on their own initiative, and it held up Brazilian emanciaption as a model of peace, good sense, and gradualism. Part of the evidence was the Rio Branco Law, which was itself a statistical trick. It provided that any person born to a slave woman would be free from the moment of his or her birth. Thereafter, as slaves died, slavery would die with them. But the law also provided that children born to a slave mother were to be held as *ingenuos* until the age of twenty-one. The rights of an *inguenuo* were exactly the same as those of a slave, so that an *ingenuo* born in 1872 could not gain real freedom until 1893, and slavery would continue for some into the 1920s.

Spain had passed a similar law for Cuba and Puerto Rico in 1870, with similar consequences, but Brazil and the Spanish Caribbean were demographically different in the nineteenth century. As an old slaveholding region, Brazil had a large enough group of Brazilian-born slaves by the 1870s to have a self-sustaining slave population – indeed, one that grew slightly over the period 1873–8. In Cuba, on the other hand, so many slaves were imported from Africa in the middle decades of the nineteenth century that the old plantation pattern of net natural decrease continued until well after the Emancipation Act of 1886.

Brazil: differential regional growth

Just as slave emanciaption was a regional issue in the United States, it was a regional issue in Brazil, but in a very different way. In Brazil, coffee was enormously profitable, and sugar production in the old northeast was not. The result was not only differential wealth but also the movement of people, and the slave trade from the northeast to the central region had important social consequences beyond the mere population movement. Slave buyers in the northeast tended to look for young males of working age. This meant that a planter in the northeast who sold off only a third of his labor force had in fact sold the only part that was economically valuable. It was to his interest to emancipate the rest – or very little to his interest not to emancipate them. Between 1874 and 1884, interregional trade from the northeast removed some 28,000 slaves, or 6 percent of the total number, and subsequent manumissions in the northeast brought the total reduction in slaves registered to 31 percent. That decrease included ficitious emancipations under the Rio Branco Law, but the equivalent loss for the coffee-growing provinces in south-central Brazil was only 9 percent. The rest of the loss came from manumitting slaves of little value. In 1871, distinct regional interest came out clearly in the vote of the Chamber of Deputies on the Rio Branco Law. The deputies from the northeast voted 36 to 6 in favor of the law; those from the south-central provinces voted 30 to 12 against.

Other regional differences emerged *within* the coffee-growing provinces. Coffee growing advanced as a moving frontier that began near the coast and fanned out into Minas Gerais and São Paulo, with the oldest plantations mainly in eastern São Paulo and rural Rio De Janeiro. By the 1870s, the earliest planters faced serious competition from the plantations farther out. Their soil was less productive than it had been. They had become technically backward, disregarding the new labor saving devices for drying and transporting the coffee beans. Though they were hard pressed, they also tended to be adamant on the question of slavery.

The planters closer to the frontier had slaves too, but they wanted to expand onto still newer land. For that, the existing stock of slaves was not enough. They began to consider alternative

Figure 14.1 Sugar and coffee planting in nineteenth-century Brazil. (From Robert Conrad, *The Destruction of Brazilian Slavery*, Berkeley: University of California Press, 1972, frontispiece. Used with permission.)

sources of labor, and they used whatever laborsaving devices they could find. On the question of emancipation, they were opposed from conviction, but they were willing to give in if necessary – if only because emancipation would make it easier to attract labor from Europe.

In the last analysis, emancipation was a provincial, not a

national, issue, and Brazilian diversity was well illustated in the way legal emancipation came to each province. From the mid-1880s on, each faced its own crisis, pushed by legal and quasi-legal action from emancipationists, often with backing from parts of the army. The crisis first became serious in Ceará, in the north, where a prolonged drought had seriously reduced the value of slaves. The emancipationists first passed legislation to block the export of slaves by sea, which reduced slave prices still further. Popular pressure for voluntary emancipation was then so successful that, between 1882 and 1884, the owners liberated virtually all the slaves remaining in the province – about 23,000 people.

At the federal level in the early 1880s, the reformers were able to pass some ameliorative measures. One of these, a law abolishing whipping in 1886, brought on the final crisis. Slaves throughout the country began running away, often with help from emancipationists. Some slaveholders began freeing their slaves voluntarily to prevent their running, hoping to save the year's crop. This too affected different provinces differently.

The crisis reached São Paulo in 1886 and 1887. Organized emancipationists gained control of the city government in Santos and made it a refuge for slaves whom they had encouraged to run away from the plantations. Such encouragement was illegal, but the provincial government failed to act; it was not really secure in its command over the army, much of which had been radicalized. The slaveholders then tried to save the crop by voluntary emancipation. It worked; the crop was saved; the transition to wage labor began, and with it came massive immigration from Europe. By 1887, only 107,000 slaves were registered in São Paulo, and in that year alone, 90,000 European immigrants entered into the province.

After that, with slavery virtually ended in the most important coffee province, the central government had no reason to hold out against legal emancipation. In 1888, the Chamber of Deputies voted an unconditional end of slavery, recognizing that de facto emancipation had already taken place. De facto slavery, however, was just as possible as de facto emancipation, and the reality of slavery often continued for years after its legal end; but the corner had been turned.

Sugar in Cuba

Cuban economic history in the nineteenth century was very different from that of Brazil, in spite of similarities in the timing of emancipation. Whereas Brazil had been an early center of the South Atlantic economy, Cuba had been a backwater until nearly the end of the eighteenth century. At that point, Cuba had a self-sustaining settler population from Europe, a self-sustaining slave population from Africa, and large group of free Afro-Cubans of mixed race. Cuba also had plenty of excellent flat land to be developed, which meant that new plantations could be laid out from scratch to use the best sugar technology in the Western world. Even as early as 1800, Cuban plantations were a little larger than contemporaneous Jamaican estates – the largest producing about 500 tons of sugar a year. By the 1850s, the *average* Cuban plantation produced 600 tons, and the largest produced 2,000 to 3,000 tons.

Cuba remained a Spanish colony after the rest of Spanish America went for independence. Perhaps because it missed the violence of the wars for independence, it was a leader in Latin American economic development. In 1837, Cubans built the first Latin American railroad line, from Havana to Guïnes, only seven years after the first U.S. railroad. During the first half of the nineteenth century, Cuba built more miles of railroad than any other country in Latin America – not more miles per unit of territory, more total miles. Even today, Cuba has the best railway network in the Americas between the United States and Argentina. This railway building fitted a strong export bias in the Cuban economy. The lines were built to serve the sugar industry, and sugar's gowth was truly spectacular. In about 1770, Cuba produced half as much sugar as Brazil. A century later, it produced nearly half the total cane sugar entering trade.

Technological advance came first in the milling and initial refining machinery. The changes began in the 1820s with larger mills and new horizontal rollers to replace the old vertical set – passing the cane through several sets of rollers to maximize the extraction of juice. New boiling equipment economized on time and fuel by using vacuum pans, in which reduced air pressure allowed the cane juice to boil at a lower temperature. But these economies came only with larger factories taking cane from a much larger area. The old two-wheeled cane carts pulled by oxen began to give way to light tramways of steel rails, with wagons pulled either by oxen or by people. The new railways and tramways opened vast stretches of inland cane land.

One stereotype about slavery is that owners have no incentive to economize on labor, but Cuban planters of the nineteenth century used the latest equipment available. For the old-style, eighteenth-century sugar estate the rule of thumb was one acre of land and one slave to produce one ton of sugar annually. By the 1830s in Cuba, this had doubled. By the 1860s, production was in the range of six to eight tons per worker on the best estates and two to four tons even on the smaller or older plantations. Technological advance and the high rate of capital investment continued down to the end of the century and the end of Spanish rule. The 1890s, indeed, marked the beginning of really large central factories that could process the cane from tens of thousands of acres. It was also the beginning of heavy North American investment that was to make Cuba an economic satellite of the United States.

Emancipation in Cuba

In Cuba two major transitions took place simultaneously in the second half of the nineteenth century. One was the mechanization of sugar production and manufacture. The second was the shift from slave labor to wage labor. Both took place in a setting of regional diversity and intense regional rivalry, and independence from Spain was always a possibility for the future.

External pressure against slavery and the intellectual conviction that slavery was wrong had nearly the same components in Cuba as in Brazil – including the enlistment of racism on the antislavery side and the association of slavery with lack of civilization among nations. Cuba also had the United States on its doorstep – another slave state up to 1865 but antislavery thereafter – and it had the further complication of Spain as the ultimate sovereign. The politics of emancipation had to be played out in two political fora, one in Madrid and the other in Havana.

Cuba's regional differences in economic growth were also

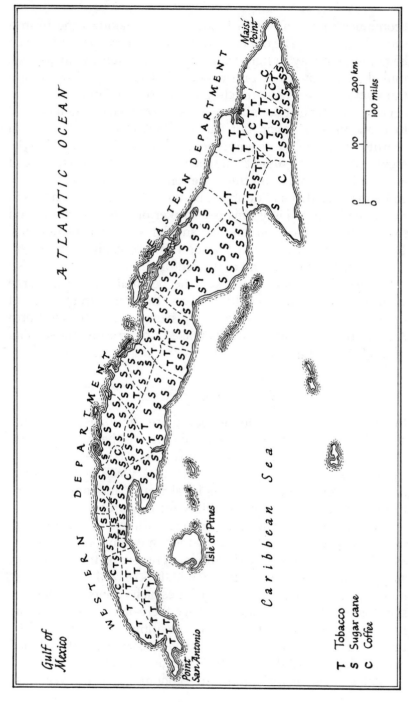

Figure 14.2 Distribution of crops in Cuba, 1857. (From Franklin Knight, *Slave Society in Cuba During the Nineteenth-Century*, Madison: University of Wisconsin Press, 1970, p. 66. Used with permission.)

distinct from those of Brazil. It was not so much the balance of growth in one region against stagnation in another, as it was different kinds of growth in different regions simultaneously. The revolution that knocked out Saint Domingue as a major sugar supplier also opened new opportunities for minor crops like tobacco and coffee. As a result, the Cuban slave population doubled in response to the sugar revolution, but the European settler population also doubled in response to other opportunities in tobacco and coffee. These immigrants came mainly from Spain and the Canary Islands, partly lured by new opportunities in the Antilles, partly pushed by hard times in the old country.

Once in Cuba, the free immigrants fitted themselves into existing Cuban social patterns. Cubans thought that tobacco farming, involving less manual labor than sugar, was as appropriate for Europeans as sugar was for Africans. European settlers with little capital could go into tobacco or cattle, even on a small holding. Thirty acres was an ordinary size for a tobacco farm worked by a dozen people or so, some of whom might be slaves. By the 1850s, Cuba had about 9,000 tobacco farms. Figure 14.2 shows that they were most common either in the far west, beyond Havana, or in the east, north of Santiago de Cuba. The cattle industry was also mainly in the east, as it is today.

Coffee plantations were larger than tobacco farms though far smaller than sugar estates. The scale was not very different from that of a North American cotton farm, about 300 acres, worked by about forty slaves and a few skilled men who might be paid workers. Sugar plantations, by contrast, often had 300 slaves or more – sometimes many more. The result is shown in Figure 14.3. Large estates with many slaves were almost entirely in the western half of the island, except for a second concentration around Guantánamo and Santiago de Cuba in the southeast.

The result was a marked social difference between regions, usually referred to as a difference between east and west, though the sugar planters around Guantánamo and Santiago were an exception in the east and tobacco growing in Pinar del Río was an exception in the far west. In 1871, nevertheless, the four main sugar districts were all in the west. They held 15 percent of the total Cuban population but 36 percent of the slaves. The four equivalent provinces in the east had 13 percent of the population but only 6 percent of the slaves.

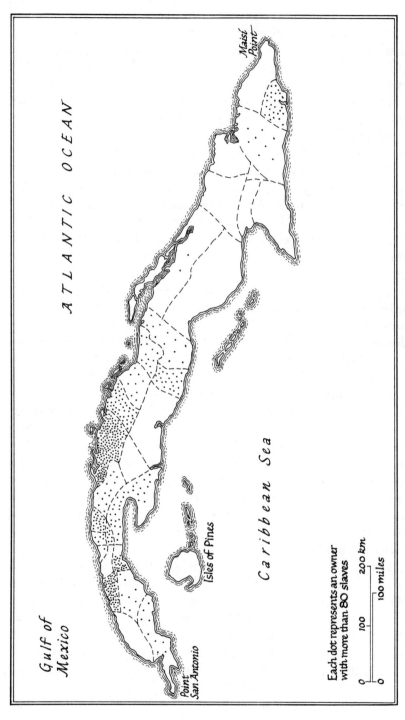

Figure 14.3 Slaveholdings in Cuba, 1857. (From Franklin Knight, *Slave Society in Cuba During the Nineteenth Century*, Madison: University of Wisconsin Press, 1970, p. 87. Used with permission.)

One result was regional tensions reflecting social tensions – a little less clear-cut than the difference between free and slave states in the United States, but important nevertheless. These implicit regional tensions increased in the second half of the century through differential growth. Up to about 1830, coffee and sugar had increased together in both Brazil and Cuba, but then Brazil moved ahead in coffee and Cuba rose to be the largest cane sugar producer in the world.

This meant, in turn, that immigration from Europe dropped off, whereas immigration through the slave trade increased. But the demographic consequence was not quite what one might expect. The newly arrived Africans were mainly male, and the Afro-Cuban rate of net natural decrease was in the expected range of about 3 to 5 percent per year, with the result that the Afro-Cuban population did not rise as fast as the number of imported slaves might suggest. Newly arrived Europeans also suffered from high initial death rates, even though the Canary Islanders and some of those from southern Spain should have had some degree of immunity to certain forms of malaria. But the Spanish immigrants had a nearly equal sex ratio. In spite of a tendency toward a net natural decrease among the newly arrived, the Euro-Cuban population continued to increase even as immigation dropped off. In 1861, as a result, the European-derived population was about 57 percent of the total, with 27 percent slave and the remaining 16 percent free people of color. In spite of the sugar revolution and heavy slave imports, the proportions were about what they had been in 1775, before the sugar revolution began.

As a result, Cuba had a white working class, living mainly outside the major sugar regions, resentful of slave owners and, to some degree, resentful of slave competition. Other tensions separated the big planters, mainly in sugar, from the smaller planters. It was the big planters who needed the continued slave trade. The smaller planters could do without it and often hired labor in any event.

The result was a set of nested conflicts between a series of metropolises and their frontiers. Madrid was the overriding metropolis, and Cuba as a whole constituted a frontier. Madrid wanted to keep Cuba a colony for reasons of national pride and revenue from Cuban taxation. Some Cubans of all social classes resented this and believed that their taxes relieved Spanish taxpayers from paying their fair share. Within Cuba, Havana and the big planters of the west-central provinces were a metropolis exercising control over the frontier of tobacco, coffee, and cattle farmers in the east and far west. The large planters were most anxious to keep slavery, which the small planters, growing less labor intensive crops, could do without.

The crisis that led to emancipation began in 1868 in Spain, where a revolution under leaders of vaguely liberal ideology deposed Queen Isabella II. The liberal victory in Spain was not sustained, but the metropolitan revolt sparked a revolt in Cuba as well – a war for Cuban independence but also a civil war, with the rebels' strength concentrated in the east, while the Spanish governors in Havana rallied the wealthy sugar planters.

This civil war, known in Cuban history as the "Ten Years' War," was no more a war to free the slaves than the American Civil War had been, but it had that result. From the point of view of Madrid, the slavery issue was partly humanitarian, though it had international implications. France, Britain, and the United States were all pressing Spain to emancipate the slaves. If any of these powers were to take the rebels' side, Cuba was lost. In 1868, the Spanish government came out with its own legislation foreshadowing the Rio Branco Law; all slaves born after 1868 were to be freed. The planter-influenced government in Cuba refused to enforce it. The Cuban rebels then encouraged slaves to run away and join them, promising emancipation. Not to be outdone, the government side also granted emancipation to slaves who joined it, though the numbers were smaller. The best of the rebel generals, António Maceo, was also an Afro-Cuban, which gave a slight emancipationist aura to the rebellion, though emancipation was not central to his aims.

In the end, the Spanish government had nothing to gain by taking a firm stand for slavery and something to gain in the hope that emancipation would help them pacify the island. Beginning in 1870, it issued a new series of laws designed to begin a transition, emancipating the newborn but leaving them under their masters up to the age of twenty-one. The real progress toward emancipation during the Ten Years' War, however, was a multitude of individual emancipations that both sides granted to slaves who joined them. The Cuban slave population dropped by 37 percent during those ten years. The Spanish government confirmed these individual acts and, in 1880, organized a transitional apprenticeship system that was to last for eight years.

By the early 1880s, a low world price for sugar had depressed the sugar industry. The demand for labor was low, and individual emancipations continued. In 1886, the government gave up and freed the comparatively few slaves who remained – about 30,000, or less than 3 percent of the population. Thus the official Emancipation Act in Cuba, as in Brazil, merely confirmed a process that had largely taken place.

These two last emancipations were therefore quite different from the end of slavery in the bloody rebellion of Saint Domingue, from that imposed by victorious federal armies in the United States, and even from the emancipations forced on unwilling colonists by metropolitan power in the French and British West Indies.

The emancipation of the slaves in Cuba in 1886 and Brazil in 1888 marked the formal end of the plantation complex. In one way, it was the last gasp of a system that had already begun to disintegrate a century earlier. Its real vitality disappeared with British emancipation in the 1830s. From another point of view, the formal end was an end of the form – not the reality. Coolie labor migrations still fed plantation regimes on the coast of Peru and elsewhere. Indian migration under contracts depriving workers of real freedom was to continue into the twentieth century, and the social practices, class power, and class weakness of the plantation regime lasted in many places through the interwar period and finally ended only in the 1940s and the early postwar years.

Suggestions for further reading

Bethell, Leslie, *The Abolition of the Brazilian Slave Trade: Britain, Brazil, and the Slave Trade Question, 1870–1869* (Cambridge: Cambridge University Press, 1970).

Conrad, Robert, *The Destruction of Brazilian Slavery* (Berkeley: University of California Press, 1972).

Knight, Franklin, *Slave Society in Cuba During the Nineteenth Century* (Madison: University of Wisconsin Press, 1970).

Moreno Franginals, Manuel, *The Sugarmill: The Socioeconomic Complex of Sugar in Cuba* (New York: Monthly Review Press, 1976).

Scott, Rebecca J., *Slave Emancipation in Cuba: The Transition to Free Labor, 1860–1899* (Princeton: Princeton University Press, 1985).

Retrospect

A collection of essays like this one can have no conclusion, but it may be worth trying to evaluate the plantation complex and its place in world history. It was clearly an important system of interrelated economic enterprises, with important ramifications for the European and North American economies – as well as for those on either side of the tropical Atlantic. It was the main impetus behind the Atlantic slave trade, the largest preindustrial population movement in the history of the world. The mature plantations of the Americas were the most specialized economies of their size yet to appear or to depend on goods carried over such great distances – inputs in food, labor, and supplies; outputs in tropical staples. It is obvious that the Europeans who ran the complex learned a great deal from the experience – in ocean shipping, tropical agriculture, and economic management at a distance. All this is a part of the background of the industrial age.

Still, it seems unlikely that the plantation complex was in any direct sense a *cause*, much less *the* cause, of the Industrial Revolution. Industrialization had its roots elsewhere, in technological change and patterns of investment in Europe itself. The complex was nevertheless a very important component of the overseas economy for France, the Netherlands, and Great Britain in the eighteenth century and into the nineteenth. In the mid-eighteenth century, Caribbean trade was about a third of French foreign and colonial trade by value, and the value of reexported sugar helped to pay for other French imports. Dutch shipping services helped to pay for imports in tropical produce. For the

British, about 10 to 20 percent of foreign and colonial trade was with the Caribbean and Africa. For the North American colonies, the percentages may have been even higher. The complex was, in short, a crucial part of the preindustrial economy that the Industrial Revolution swept away.

When all that is said, was the plantation complex a good thing? Would the world have been better off without it? Whatever the benefits, the costs of producing them fell on people who did not benefit, and those costs were immense. If the goal was migration, the comparatively humane method is to move people, let the first generation sustain the inevitable loss from new diseases, and then let natural population growth take its course. The plantation complex moved Europeans into Africa and the tropical Americas at enormous cost in loss of life. It moved Africans to the New World at even greater costs.

Were the benefits worth it, and to whom? Overall, the sum of individual profits from slave traders and from plantations themselves was not statistically higher than normal for other enterprises of their time and place. The capital and enterprise might just as well have been placed elsewhere. Of course, short-term profits from gold mining in Brazil, from particular plantations, and from particular voyages in the slave trade were enormous. But this fact may merely have brought into play what some economists have called the "Vegas principle." The Vegas or Klondike principle states that people will invest when they see a *chance* of high winnings, even when they know that statistically they must lose – if only because the house must take its cut and the house runs the game. For the individual players it is a less than zero-sum game.

If this suggestion is correct – that the European slave traders and planters en masse may have gained very little – was there any equivalent of the Vegas gambling house? No historians today argue seriously that Africa profited from selling its people into the slave trade, though particular monarchs and traders no doubt gained from their part in capturing or transporting others. It would be equally hard to argue that slavery and the slave trade were, on margin, beneficial to Brazil or the Caribbean. Other, slower forms of development would certainly have given at least as good a chance of creating a juster and richer society than the one that did emerge. Europe as a whole might have gained, but those who died as sailors in the slave trade or as soldiers in the West Indies have to be taken into account, and evidence of a net economic gain from total investment is weak. The only likely equivalent of the Las Vegas "house" was the European public. They got cheaper sugar and cheaper coffee than they might have had otherwise, though nuritionists are far from certain that increased sugar consumption was a net gain.[1] Even if it were, it is hard to argue that the benefit to European diets was worth the investment in lives and treasure that it finally cost.

[1] For discussion, see Sidney W. Mintz, *Sweetness and Power: The Place of Sugar in Modern History* (New York: Viking Press, 1985), pp. 74–150.

Appendix

Table 1. *Brazilian and Caribbean slave prices (in pounds sterling) 1640–1830*

Decade	Brazil	West Indies
1640s	31	17
1650s	31	26
1660s	29	21
1670s	27	21
1680s	16	21
1690s	14	24
1700s	24	25
1710s	44	25
1720s	44	24
1730s	44	24
1740s	33	28
1750s	29	33
1760s	18	37
1770s	22	40
1780s	28	43
1790s	28	53
1800s	30	53
1810s	35	
1820s	54	

Note: Prices are the mean of the range for each period. West Indian prices are represented by Jamaica alone to the 1680s. Brazilian prices for the 1660s have been determined by interpolation.

Source: Joseph C. Miller, "Slave Prices in the Portuguese Southern Atlantic," in Paul E. Lovejoy (ed.), *Africans in Bondage* (Madison: University of Wisconsin African Studies Program, 1986), p. 70.

Table 2. *Slave prices in Africa (in current pounds sterling)*

Decade	Luanda	Gold Cost	Senegal
1700s	6.2	12.6	7.5
1710s	9.8	16.8	9.7
1720s	11.3	14.2	7.5
1730s	11.3	20.2	11.7
1740s	14.1	17.7	12.8
1750s	14.1	17.7	12.8
1760s	11.8	20.0	16.2
1770s	13.5	16.2	17.9
1780s	14.9	29.1	24.1
1790s	17.7	25.3	27.5
1800s	15.8	23.5	
1810s	17.0		
1820s	24.9		

Note: Some interpretation for missing data. When prices are reported as a range of values, the mean is listed.
Source: Joseph C. Miller, "Slave Prices in the Portuguese South Atlantic, 1600–1830," in Paul E. Lovejoy (ed.), *Africans in Bondage* (Madison: University of Wisconsin African Studies Program, 1986), p. 67.

Table 3. *Eighteenth-century slave exports from Africa and from representative regions (in annual average exports, 000s)*

Decade	West-Central Africa	Bight of Biafra	Senegambia	Total exports
1701–10	80.1	10.0	18.4	312.2
1711–20	72.0	10.0	30.9	349.4
1721–30	115.5	4.5	22.5	398.0
1731–40	177.3	45.1	26.2	522.3
1741–50	189.2	71.3	25.0	536.2
1751–60	195.6	100.7	22.5	529.0
1761–70	220.2	126.3	14.4	635.1
1771–80	211.4	127.3	12.4	580.0
1781–90	431.1	133.8	22.1	887.7
1791–1800	365.3	185.4	7.0	763.5
Total	2057.7	814.4	201.4	5,513.4

Source: Paul E. Lovejoy, *Transformations in Slavery* (Cambridge: Cambridge University Press, 1983), p. 50.

Table 4. *West African imports in the era of the slave trade*

Commodity	Column 1 (%)[a]	Column 2 (%)[b]
Metal and metalware	22.4	5.4
European textiles	42.5	25.0
Indian textiles	18.3	33.9
Weapons and gunpowder	6.4	9.8
Beads and jewelry	3.1	8.8
Cowrie shells	7.2	
Spirits		7.1
Tobacco		10.0
Total	99.9	100.0

[a]Exports to Africa by the Royal African Company, 1680–2 (minor items disregarded).
[b]Imports into Senegambia, annual averages, 1831–40 (minor items disregarded).
Source: Philip D. Curtin, *Economic Change in Precolonial Africa* (Madison: University of Wisconsin Press, 1975), pp. 313, 318.

Index